The Faber Book of Modern Australian Verse

The Faber Book of
Modern Australian Verse

Edited by Vincent Buckley

faber and faber

LONDON · BOSTON

First published in 1991
by Faber and Faber Limited
3 Queen Square London WC1N 3AU

Photoset by Wilmaset Birkenhead Wirral
Printed in England by
Clays Ltd, St Ives plc

A CIP record for this book is available from the British Library

ISBN 0-571-15064-0

Contents

Introduction   xv
Publisher's Note   xxxiv

John Shaw Neilson (1872–1942)
The Orange Tree   1
Colour Yourself for a Man   2
The Sun Is Up   3
Stony Town   4
Take Down the Fiddle, Karl!   5

Kenneth Slessor (1901–71)
The Night-Ride   7
Wild Grapes   7
Talbingo   8
Country Towns   9
North Country   9
South Country   10
Five Bells   11
An Inscription for Dog River   15
Beach Burial   16

R. D. Fitzgerald (1902–87)
Long Since . . .   17
The Face of the Waters   18
from Eleven Compositions: Roadside   20
The Wind at Your Door   22

A. D. Hope (1907–   )
Easter Hymn   27
The Gateway   27
Ascent into Hell   28
The Pleasure of Princes   30
The Death of the Bird   31
The Coasts of Cerigo   32
Advice to Young Ladies   34
Lament for the Murderers   36
Loving Kind   37
Inscription for a War   38

Elizabeth Riddell (1909–)
The Letter   39
Forebears   40

William Hart-Smith (1911–)
Fishing   44
Bathymeter   44
Birth   45
Ambrosia   45
Observation   46
Altamira   47

Douglas Stewart (1913–85)
from Glencoe   49
The Night of the Moths   50
The Silkworms   50
B Flat   51

John Blight (1913–)
Cormorants   53
Mangrove   53
Conflagration   54
The Disarrayed   55

Kenneth Mackenzie (1913–55)
The Snake   57
Caesura   58
Two Trinities   58
An Old Inmate   60

John Manifold (1915–85)
For Comrade Katharine   62
The Last Scab of Hawarth   63
Fife Tune   64
Fencing School   65
The Tomb of Lt John Learmonth, AIF   65

[vi]

David Campbell (1915–79)
Men in Green   68
Who Points the Swallow   69
from Works and Days   70
from Starting from Central Station   71
Sugar Loaf   72
Landfall   72
Portents over Coffee   73
from Two Songs with Spanish Burdens   74

Judith Wright (1915–   )
The Hawthorn Hedge   76
Woman to Man   77
The Garden   77
Train Journey   78
Old House   79
For Precision   80
The Curtain   80
To Another Housewife   81
Against the Wall   82
Pro and Con   83
Smalltown Dance   83
from For a Pastoral Family   85

James McAuley (1917–76)
Dialogue   87
Jesus   87
from The Hero and the Hydra   88
Father, Mother, Son   88
Against the Dark   89
One Tuesday in Summer   90
Autumn in Hobart   91
Parish Church   91

Anne Elder (1918–76)
Seen Out   92
Crazy Woman   93
Yarra Park   96

Singers of Renown 97
To a Friend under Sentence of Death 97

Gwen Harwood (1920–)
Prize-Giving 99
Boundary Conditions 100
In the Park 101
Person to Person 102
Dust to Dust 103
Winter Quarters 104
Looking towards Bruny 105
Dialogue 106
Mother Who Gave Me Life 107

Rosemary Dobson (1920–)
from Daily Living 109

Dimitris Tsaloumas (1921–)
An Extravagant Lover's Note of Explanation 111
The Grudge 113

Alexander Craig (1923–)
The Ceiling 114
from Sea Change 114

Francis Webb (1925–73)
The Day of the Statue 116
Morgan's Country 117
For My Grandfather 118
The Gunner 118
Dawn Wind on the Islands 119
Vlamingh and Rottnest Island 120
Towards the Land of the Composer 121
A Death at Winson Green 123
Nessun Dorma 124

Vincent Buckley (1925–88)
Death in January 126

from Golden Builders   127
The Blind School   130
Your Father's House   132
Internment   133
Teaching German Literature   134

Bruce Beaver (1928–   )
from Letters to Live Poets   136
from Lauds and Plaints   144

Peter Porter (1929–   )
Once Bitten, Twice Bitten; Once Shy, Twice Shy   148
The Easiest Room in Hell   149
Non Piangere, Liù   150
Good Ghost, Gaunt Ghost   151

R. A. Simpson (1929–   )
Tram Driver's Song   152
To My Mother   152
Old Children   153

Bruce Dawe (1930–   )
Clouds   155
Husband and Wife   156
Drifters   156
Homecoming   157
Weapons Training   158
The Christ of the Abyss   159

Philip Martin (1931–   )
Nursing Home   160

Evan Jones (1931–   )
The Falling Sickness   162
Hostel   162
A Line from Keats   163
Honeymoon, South Coast   164
A Solicitors' World   165

Jennifer Strauss (1933–   )
After a Death   166
Stone, Scissors, Paper   167

Fay Zwicky (1933–   )
To a Sea-Horse   169
Dreams   170
Bat   170

Chris Wallace-Crabbe (1934–   )
Losses and Recoveries   172
The Aftermath: Yorkshire 1644   174
Childhood   175
New Carpentry   176
Death, 1976   176
Panoptics   178
Jasmine   179

David Malouf (1934–   )
The Year of the Foxes   180
Reading Horace outside Sydney: 1970   181
Off the Map   182

Randolph Stow (1935–   )
Dust   184
Ruins of the City of Hay   185
The Dying Chair   186
Sleep   187
Jimmy Woodsers   188

Thomas Shapcott (1935–   )
The Litanies of Julia Pastrana (1832–1860)   189

Les A. Murray (1938–   )
Driving through Sawmill Towns   193
from Evening Alone at Bunyah   195
An Absolutely Ordinary Rainbow   196
from Walking to the Cattle Place   197
The Broad Bean Sermon   199
The Mitchells   200

[x]

Lachlan MacQuarie's First Language 201
from The Buladelah-Taree Holiday Song Cycle 202
The Grassfire Stanzas 203
The Smell of Coal Smoke 205

Peter Steele (1939–)
Countdown 207
Element 207
Like a Ghost 208

Geoffrey Lehmann (1940–)
from Ross' Poems 209

Andrew Taylor (1940–)
Halfway to Avalon 213
Two in Search of Dawn 214

Jennifer Rankin (1941–79)
Williamstown 215
Still Water Tread 216

Roger McDonald (1941–)
Grasshopper 217
Bachelor Farmer 218
Others 219

John Tranter (1943–)
Sonnet 63 *from* Crying in Early Infancy 220
Butterfly 220
At the Criterion 221

Robert Adamson (1944–)
Action Would Kill It / A Gamble 223
Wade in the Water 224
My Granny 224
My First Proper Girlfriend 225
from Growing Up Alone 226
My Afternoon 227

Robert Gray (1945–)
Journey: the North Coast   228
A Kangaroo   229
'The Single Principle of Forms'   230
North Coast Town   230
The Sea-Shell   231
Sketch of the Harbour   232
Landscape   233

Christine Churches (1945–)
Neighbour   234
Divination   235
Late Summer Storm   235
Grandmother's Ninetieth Birthday   236
I Wonder What Went of Him   237
Walking in the Lambing Paddock   238

Rhyll McMaster (1947–)
Slanted World   239
Fire Screen   240
Bird of Glass   241
Dream in an Afternoon   242
A Dream of Washed Hair   242
Washing the Money   243
Seven in the Morning   243
Eeling   244

Martin Johnston (1947–1990)
Aristarchus and the Whale   246
The Scattering Layer   247

Michael Dransfield (1948–73)
Pioneer Lane   248
The Grandfather   249
Presences   250

John Forbes (1950–)
Rolling in Money   251
Blonde & Aussie   252

Kevin Hart (1954–   )
A Dream of France   253
This Day   253
Midsummer   254
The Real World   255
Your Shadow   255
Come Back   256

Acknowledgements   259
Index of Poets   265
Index of Titles   266
Index of First Lines   271

Introduction

Poetry has existed in Australia for thousands of years, but not in languages that many living Australians understand. People like me, descendants of the European invader settlers of the past two centuries, have a very limited access to fragments of it in translation. In that form, they are sometimes very beautiful and haunting, but in their original form they are not, or not merely, 'poems' in the usual European sense. Although I am delighted to have read such translations as exist (and I have never seen an example where there are alternative translations to choose from), I consider it unsuitable to include them in an anthology such as this. Perhaps it is time for the whole question to be debated; for they are part of the Other which still challenges the colonists who have misunderstood and demeaned it. Very few white Australians know anything of any Aboriginal language, and fewer still can translate one. For my purposes, 'Australian poetry' refers to work written in English. As it has developed over two hundred years, this is full of inner cross-influences, as well as connections with poetry from countries outside Australia – Anglophone and other. It is not a dialect poetry, and it is not possible to specify regional differences as dialectal ones. Australian English is not eccentric, and the boundaries of the country's poetry are not set by diction.

It is sometimes said (though not by Australians) that one should not speak of 'Australian poetry' at all, since the status indicated by the adjective is 'problematic'. Well, it is not part of English or American poetry; like them, it contributes to world poetry, and like them it is open in some respects and closed in others. Australian poetry is not problematic in any way that does not apply to every other country's poetry, 'national' or not. Further, the issue may be regional rather than national. The Australia in question is a site and economy of cultural activity rather than a nation-state.

Nor is it exactly a provincial poetry; for a hundred years most Australian poets have sought to set their own terms in which to develop. They have not always succeeded. For obvious reasons, it began as a derivative and dependent product, but it has shown a steady tendency to diverge from its parent models. In this century the divergence grew wider, and some Australian poets now have an international influence. But until recently Australia was, if not a province, a colony – legally of Great Britain, culturally of England. Treated as a colony, it thought and behaved as a colony, even if intermittently. It no longer does so, although the poetry is hampered by a remaining economic colonialism; and, whatever deference is still paid to English or American *arbitri elegentiarum*, poetry survives the habit of deference to assert an economy of its own.

By the late nineteenth century, the imported language had become a home language, and various aspects of Australia provided the central subjects for poetry. By the end of the century, Australia had a tradition of its own, that of the balladic lyric, a domestication of two strains which had been dominant for several decades: the lyrics and narratives of Harpur, Kendall and their successors, and the ballads, whether satirical, dramatic, or ruminative. Both strains had been here since the foundation of the colony. After Adam Lindsay Gordon the ballad literature developed to the point where, early in this century, Henry Lawson and A. B. Paterson were the leading poets in the country; and Paterson in particular was a master of mixing action with sweeping lyricism.

Critics were led to debate evolutionist and adaptationist views of the way poetry had developed, and fell into the fallacies which tend to beset accounts of new literatures. One is the fallacy of corporate development, that the poets of an emerging country learn a distinctive diction, tone, form and attitude together, develop them together, and soon become the most important influences on one another. If asked to trace 'the course of Australian poetry', one might do so in a broad way, but ought not to make too much of the trope: several 'courses' might well be running simultaneously. For example, the 'bush ballad' in the late nineteenth century created a vehemently nativist strain and helped to swing our poetry away from English models; but it too was partly associated with the forsaken models – Paterson, with Kipling, for instance. The forsaken lyric effusions did not die away altogether, but remained beside and sometimes within their supplanters; and the pluralism by now being established was extended by new growths.

When the balladic lyric failed and slackened, it was replaced by one of its own components, the moody lyric; and its decline coincided with the death of an alternative which had barely had time to announce itself, the grandiose psycho-tragedy of Christopher Brennan. This talented poet was thoroughly Europeanized, influenced by Baudelaire as well as by Mallarmé and Yeats. While he did manage to give a flavour of *fin de siècle* Sydney, the city was for Brennan the stage for an ordeal presented in almost operatic terms. His learning was and is admired, and his suffering respected; but his poetry is frequented by scholars rather than poets. His example was one to be envied and shunned.

The adoption of a corporate model seems necessary to colonial cultures seeking to establish that they are distinctive. It works better in retrospect than at the time, and is a way of constructing identity as an historical event or process which can now be assumed, and have its benefits put to use. The inevitable metaphors are 'evolve' (the poetry and its language were *destined* to develop on a Whig model of society), 'adapt' (they conform to the land which becomes their chief subject, and so make the land conform to them), 'coming of age', 'maturing', and so on. The poetry, like the nation, is almost universally thought to have sought 'a national identity', and generally agreed to have found it. Nobody asks whether *a* national identity (a notion redolent of idealistic yearnings that live by acts of will) is different from *the* national identity, so compromised by its own factuality.

The 1914–18 war produced little 'war poetry' from Australians. It had been an immense exhilaration and an immense trauma to the Australian psyche. There were the great numbers killed and wounded, all thousands of miles away; there was prolonged civil conflict within Australia over the nature of the war and the proposals to conscript people, many of whom believed the war to be none of their business; and there were other things, which caused a puzzled rethinking of 'belonging' and of identity. But there was also an official myth, rhetoric and excitement – the idea of 'growing up' and 'coming of age', which combined with those curious notions, so common at the time, of 'being blooded' and 'having a baptism of fire'. These ideas were internalized by large numbers of individual Australians. Australians who came back from the foreign holocaust to the local drabness did not write Apocalypses. If modernism was to become seeded here, it would not be in those terms.

Certainly there were major changes in the 1920s and 1930s, but did they occur through the taking up of that set of habits and expectations which in other countries were said to be symptoms of 'modernism' or, in alternative versions, of 'the modern'? The answer generally given is yes, and it is generally supplemented with the claim that the new poetry asserts a new national self-sufficiency. These claims are questionable. It *is* true that a proto-modernism developed here, much as it developed in England and America, a view which sought to include international perspectives, and which stressed oriental and exotic references, used demotic speech and attitudes, worked for speech rhythms, and tried to incorporate vignettes of city life. But these were timid experiments, and what succeeded them was not the daring adventurism of Pound and Eliot, but something much more constrained and, perhaps, programmatic.

As with other countries, making it new in Australia involved poets in taking large leaps into the past for exemplars who had *not* influenced their Victorian and Edwardian predecessors, among whom Brennan must be counted. The trainer and chief athlete was Norman Lindsay (prolific as writer, painter and illustrator from before the First World War until well after the 1930s), who combined in the one aesthetic an insistence on the Europeanization of art, the peopling of Australian landscapes with figures from classical mythology, attacks on the philistine morality known in Australia as 'wowserism', and an association of art with sexual power. It was a programme for a form of vitalism, which could have gone in the direction either of a new realism or of a new fantasy. Lindsay himself tended towards fantasy, though his chief disciples among the poets gradually found that their fanciful excursions did not fully express their sense of the world. The large leap into the past was not into Yeats's Byzantium, or the Middle Ages of Pound, or Cathay, or Norse or Anglo-Saxon cultures, but into the flesh-world of the High Renaissance, the exuberant world preoccupied with forms of display which had their echo in the Romanticism of three hundred years later. In poetry it involved a form of hectic impressionism.

Australia still had in the 1920s no body of city poetry, perhaps because it had no cities in the way Paris and London were cities. When 'Furnley Maurice' wrote of Melbourne he adopted the position of genial observer, and gave one poem the significantly joshing title, 'The Victoria Markets Recollected in Tranquillity'. When Kenneth Slessor began to write of Sydney, it was in forms of exuberant fantasy; the city and its harbours were a place of illusion, imaginings, alternative consciousness, a wholesale rejection of everyday. Not till death entered the frame did his poetry change to accommodate the everyday as well as the red-soft night.

It is necessary to mention Slessor so early; for if some deep development occurred here before the Second World War, a change which precipitated other changes and coloured the whole terrain, it probably occurred in the 1920s and 1930s, and Slessor and Fitzgerald were responsible for it. It was from them that the first signs arose of what some critics still identify as 'modernism'; and most retrospective accounts try to fit it into the general evolutionist and the general nativist pictures: it is to be the result of a genuine development, but it is also to strengthen Australian autonomy and self-sufficiency. It is the proof that we had developed a modernism as radical as everyone else's, but at the same time had come more firmly of age; we had changed radically to match everyone else, and we had radically confirmed our uniqueness; we had moved closer to general acceptability and closer to national freedom. But innovations do not have to be 'modernist'; and distinctiveness does not have to issue in a group movement.

These are the poets whom H. M. Green in his monumental history calls 'the intellectuals', comparing Fitzgerald for example with Donne, the connection presumably being Eliot. Green and others saw Fitzgerald and Slessor as the heirs of T. S. Eliot, and their methods local adaptations of his. Pound was rarely mentioned, although 'Furnley Maurice' was evidently sponsoring his poetry to Melbourne audiences in 1918. The later Pound was not claimed as a precursor by any significant poet. The persistent references to Eliot also seem misleading: whatever arrived through Slessor and Fitzgerald, it was not 'modernism', but something more consonant with the way Australia was.

The uncertainty about whether Australian poetry now followed its own established road or watercourse, or whether it was managing to be both modernist and nativist, was a sign that nothing decisive had in fact happened; and the preoccupation with coming of age was a sign that Australia was an uncertain, partly developed, dependent country, vigorously asserting tentative virtues. Both then and later, many critics inhibited national self-awareness for the sake of promoting a nationalist stereotype.

This is in keeping with the history of colonial and post-colonial poetries in this century: Canada, New Zealand and South Africa may all have experienced the change that leads to changes, but none of them developed a modernist poetry powerful enough, at the relevant time, to represent their national versions of the international movement. Their poetries changed, 'progressed' even, in a less abrupt and dramatic way, representing a more flexible version than had been available before of the national terrain. And if you left it for thirty years before you tried to follow the great initiating modernist experiments, they would clearly be redundant. There is no point in the late arrival of the avant-garde.

In so far as modernism affected Australian poetry in the 1920s and 1930s, it was in terms of local technique, not of deep technique with its implication that the world and language were being rethought and refelt. The surfaces changed, but no Australian poet saw the need to experiment with the depths of the psyche in the pursuit of wholly new orders of language.

[xx]

Ruling conventions were not split apart in order to radicalize forms and ideas of form. The poets stood by conventions and extended them. There was speculation, and free-ranging experiment, but they avoided serious formal dislocation, and they were exercised on traditional concerns: explorers and exploring, seafarers, long voyages, and freaks of chance, pioneers, settlers, genealogies, oddities of history, dramatic confrontations, impressions of natural effects, the land and its fauna. Only in isolated pockets was it a metropolitan poetry.

The truth is, the radical individualism required of modernist experiments would have run counter to some Australian need for poets to prove themselves as a group, and to establish a new poetry not by revolutionary example but by agreement, consensus. This is shown by the degree of acceptance achieved by Fitzgerald and Slessor: their enterprise felt right.

Fitzgerald's productiveness and Slessor's short creative life may suggest that the latter crept modestly into poetic fame at the heels of the former. Such an impression is the reverse of the truth. In retrospect, the growth of Slessor's dominance is evident, phase by phase. Down the two post-war decades, he published books in 1923, 1924, 1926, 1931, 1932, 1933 , and in 1939 *Five Bells*. Fitzgerald, publishing in 1926 and 1927, was an altogether slower and more considered producer at that time, and it is odd to realize that his most important, certainly his largest, works are from the 1940s and later – written, that is, after Slessor had given up writing poetry for good. When he *did* publish, it might be a pamphlet-poem or an epic about dynastic wars in the Pacific. His pace of growth was on an altogether different scale. For all the appearance of sheer play and improvisation, Slessor was actually producing neat, crisp, cadenced poems. Fitzgerald was overlong not by miscalculation but by design. He was the servant of the story he wanted to tell, a long story, the story of a long backwardness. So it is Slessor who dominates the revival of between-wars, contemporary now with pioneers such as John Shaw Neilson or Lawson, now with the young Kenneth Mackenzie or John Thompson. And Mary Gilmore, Paterson and Hugh McCrae appear with the regularity of survivors, heartening the work.

Certainly, too, Slessor's modest if vital and distinctive

innovations came into a receptive environment. The currency of Norman Lindsay and his talented son Jack, who was associated with Slessor in the 1920s before he left for London, the high reputation of Hugh McCrae, and Slessor's own reputation among the Sydney journalists who constituted Bohemia and provided an audience – all of these made the progress of poetic revolution a painless and cheerful one. Christopher Brennan too had lived in that Arcadia of Bohemia, but his self-shaping grandeur had not suited its need for general fellowship. Slessor and Fitzgerald were, in a sense, exactly what was called for.

They came into a world in which the reigning poets were still active, but in some decline. C. J. Dennis and A. B. ('Banjo') Paterson had immense readerships; one celebrated the free demotic larrikin spirit of the city's slums, the other celebrated the free, musical nativist spirit of the bush; one showed callow youth, the other several ages of shrewd man. Both created what Australians call 'characters': distinctive, assertive and amusing individuals. Mary Gilmore, veteran of the failed Utopian experiment in Paraguay, was still writing, and was to write for several more decades; her poetry barely changed over that time, and although she was much loved I could never see it as matching her legendary self. John Shaw Neilson was writing, and was to write in near blindness into the late 1930s; his poetry too barely changed, and is praised now for the same reasons as sixty years ago.

These poets and others, bush balladists and lyricists, were sustained by the same journals which supported the new poets. Chief of these was the Sydney *Bulletin*, which published Fitzgerald and those, like Francis Webb, whom he influenced in the next generation. Fitzgerald and Slessor were praised for newness, for intellectuality, but they had an appeal to something already dominant in the intellectual culture, something colourful, plastic and fey, something almost un-intellectual. But there were no other claimants to be pioneers of modernism in Australia; and so Browning came into his own on distant shores, with his penchant for gesture and confrontation.

James McAuley, with a collaborator, Harold Stewart, sabotaged the only full-scale effort to set up a modernist movement in Australia. The attempt had been made in the 1940s by Max Harris and his collaborators in the magazine *Angry Penguins*, which was quite unusual in Australia, and pretty unusual anywhere, for its readiness to attempt what others merely proclaimed, an avante-garde across the entire front of the arts. *Angry Penguins* was concerned with the visual arts, jazz, experimental dancing, philosophy, psychiatry, Marxist and anarchist approaches to social revolution, and of course poetry. It published American, English and European work as well as Australian; it acted out the fundamental modernist conviction that the avant-garde lies across the boundaries of countries as well as of art forms; so it was international in that it sought overseas connections, not just overseas recognition or validation. It introduced modernism in poetry at perhaps the romantic end of the spectrum, where surrealism and symbolism flourished; it published Dylan Thomas and Henry Treece, for example. Its short life was ended by the hoax which first created an anarchist poet, Ern Malley, induced Harris to accept him as a genius, then publicized the hoax in hostile and contemptuous terms: Harris was prosecuted for obscenity. It is no wonder that most poets found Judith Wright, or even McAuley, safer to follow than Ern Malley, or Rilke, or Breton. The fall of this modernism occurred about the time Wright and McAuley were just coming into their strength. The destructiveness involved in this affair is by now notorious.

Naturally, some of the new energy released by the 1920s and 1930s went into the imagining of origins, as is common in colonial countries. The near-desert of the outback was soon matched by the wilderness of the oceans. Where Dennis and Paterson had dealt with what seemed archetypal behaviour, the modernized poets experimented with a group of interests, stories and types which seemed to come from a common root: sea discovery, land settlement, and continental exploration. These gradually diverged from the common root, since they were separate tasks and involved different psychological ordeals; soon, it could be said, poets were specializing in one or another. Slessor, William Hart-Smith and Douglas Stewart specialized in sea-discovery. Judith Wright, Mary Gilmore and David Campbell wrote of land settlement, as in a sense Paterson and Lawson had already done; and Francis Webb, after turning to the light the ambiguous figure of Ben Boyd, discoverer, speculator and settler, entered the agonized darkness of the land explorers, Leichhardt and Eyre. James McAuley's *Captain Quiros* was an attempt to put the themes of sea discovery on a new, Catholic basis; and in addition he and A. D. Hope raised the 'matter of Australia', asking whether Australia was a degeneration of Europe, or a repetition, or a mockery.

In Webb's hands, the theme of land exploration was used both to show extreme psychic and physical stress, and to develop poetic form: the madness of mirage shown in theatrical sequences. Webb was also interested in the psychotic aloneness of the bushranger Morgan. So the outback, more than the ocean, stayed inside the mythic picture of Australian poets as a place of absurd and heroic suffering. Sporadically the lore and the actual condition of the Aboriginal peoples were explored, in the work of Rex Ingamells, Roland Robinson and Ian Mudie, with particular statements by Gilmore and Wright. It is doubtful how deep they could go, but they were very serious; so the outback perimeters were broadened.

None of these experiments, important as some of them were, ever tried to develop a formal means of developing history as a process. Images of theatre, spectacle, gesture and suspense were the dominant ones, in the work of poets from Fitzgerald to Webb. Indeed, Webb's long sequence on Leichhardt is called 'Leichhardt in Theatre'. Douglas Stewart turned to poetic drama for *Ned Kelly* and other plays. Much later, David Campbell implied theatre and spectatorship in *Deaths and Pretty Cousins*. The past was being carefully framed; but costume drama lived somewhere inside the images. It was a recurrent tendency over several decades, and of course it was anti-'modernist' in effect, although its methods were overtly experimental.

These habits of theatricalizing the past were decisively challenged with the arrival of Les A. Murray in the 1960s; for Murray, the country's past was centred on his family's past, which he saw in mythic terms, so that, while being both subjective and colourful, it also seemed representative – not of important long-documented grazing families but of the small, often desperate, 'cocky' farmers of the east coast. Such poetry was a rhetorical exercise in self-assertion, but it had a clearly visualized social base. Poems like Mackenzie's 'An Old Inmate' had preceded him in this, as had Judith Wright's seminal 'South of My Days'. But they were breaking into an artistic world in which poems had to have story and presence, echoes of the stage drama and flickers of prose fiction.

In the 1930s a resurgence of prose fiction sent poetry somewhat to the margins; the rush of novels in the late 1930s was not matched by a rush of poetry, and what books of verse were published were by well-known and frequently old poets. From 1939, most younger poets were in the armed forces; but in 1943 and 1944, with the fortunes of war turning, the wave of poetry turned too: Hart-Smith, Stewart, Rosemary Dobson, Geoffrey Dutton, Kenneth Mackenzie, John Manifold and Ern Malley all joined the familiar names. Selecteds and Collecteds began to appear. But 1946 was the *annus mirabilis*, with first books by Wright and McAuley, with Manifold's *Selected Verse*, volumes by Hart-Smith and Stewart and anthologies edited by Mackaness and H. M. Green, which set targets for a new generation. It was an inaugurating year, and the rest of the decade set the standard which later decades, for all their triumphalism, have to meet. Those years, up to 1952, saw several of the poets I have mentioned at the height of their powers: Robinson and Fitzgerald writing abundantly, McAuley (if not writing much) meditating a new poetic, and Hope collecting his confidence and his poems for a triumphant entry to be made later, in 1955.

The modernizing influences in Australia between 1930 and 1960 were not Pound or Williams or Stevens, and only marginally Eliot; they were Yeats and Auden. In the later part of that period the situation was complicated by 'neo-Romantic' pieces of modernism coming from Britain and America, and also by the no-nonsense contemporaneity of the English 'Movement'; but these were not as powerful as some have thought, and in any case would have been anti-modernist in effect. Yeats and Auden remained steady, even growing mentors, and Auden indeed was followed in each of his stylistic phases.

Both these poets suited the compromise which Australian poetry had by now reached with 'modernism' – to convert new challenges into narrative, or quasi-narrative. While the crystal of a story could be kept near the centre of the converging images, sanity and order could be preserved whatever the nightmare. Australian poetry had come to rely on various kinds of serial progression. Fitzgerald was in a way an extreme example of this tendency; he more and more made the story element explicit, and dealt with the contradictions of civilization by showing them in human stance and choice. Slessor, with more of the painter's flair, specialized rather in composition, sought a frame for action and image rather than ways of extending them.

These traditions, stemming from Slessor and Fitzgerald and influenced often by Yeats and Auden, persisted with great strength and always claimed the centre of the field. Some poets like Judith Wright and David Campbell, who began in the 1940s, were influenced in the 1960s by new techniques, and adapted themselves to the waves lapping at them from several directions; yet they never gave ground. If any poets were to be marginalized in the confusion of modes and influences, it would not be they. On the contrary, along with Douglas Stewart, John Manifold and a few others, they were the second generation of the renewing impulse. Nearly all of them began their poetry after Slessor finished his; a pivotal date for them is the end of the Second World War. They dominated Australian poetry for two decades or more, and are still dominant in some minds. The third generation, which included Gwen Harwood, Francis Webb and Bruce Beaver, came close behind. With them, the poetry diversified radically; and with Beaver, certain late-modern influences from America proved the start of a whole new wing of poetry.

The frames of generations are interfered with, too, by the presence of those two enigmatic figures, A. D. Hope and James McAuley. The former belonged by chronology to the senior generation, that of the initiators; and though he proclaimed himself an anti-modernist, his combination of set forms with vernacular language must surely count as innovatory. The latter belonged by age with Wright and Campbell, to whose basic tendencies he seemed for years overtly hostile; yet as his lyric gift fell gently into the noble if staid melancholy of his last poems, these poets came to acknowledge him as one of themselves, and thought him more like them than in fact he was.

Hope and McAuley were 'classicists'; at least, that was the word we used at the time, in the 1950s. The basic Australian traditions were romantic – and these two were against all romanticisms, all self-aggrandizing afflatus, all false consciousness about the actual fate of human beings. In fact their self-dedication to poetry was as wildly romantic, as exuberantly or gloomily elevated, as that of any post-romantic. They were as responsible as Wright or Campbell for acclimatizing Yeats and, especially in Hope's case, Auden.

Some opinions would have it that the 1950s were claimed by a new and intrusive group, the University wits, specializing in irony, centred on Melbourne, and having a connection with the 'Movement' in England. The truth is less neat. Several poets did begin publishing in Melbourne, and their emphases were different from the ruling *mores*: yet they arose not by policy or programme but in an attempt to meet their own situation, part of which was that they could not think in terms of the ruling themes or forms, and certainly could not accept them as a prescription. Further, it was the period of the Korean War and of the Cold War generally; poets influenced by Slessor or Stewart were emotionally very remote from the issues implicit in this geo-political situation. Their poetry was in a sense public, in that it was a poetry of consensus, but in another sense it was private, opposed to protest and public involvement. Very little was written about the Korean War; and several poets made substantial reputations while hardly acknowledging the existence of the international tensions within which we lived.

This is not true of the Melbourne poets referred to. More important than their irony or their connection with universities (where either of these existed) was their awareness of the common human reality as full of threat and tension. The Cold War was ever present in the cultural discussions of Melbourne, though not only there. Manifold, David Martin and Laurence Collinson were Communists, McAuley an anti-Communist; but the discussions were not only about Communism, rather about the whole nature of political and social reality, the way myth impinges on politics, the identity of the torturers, the styles of power. R. A. Simpson, Evan Jones and Chris Wallace-Crabbe were among the poets who approached these topics; but foremost of them was Bruce Dawe. Most of these poets came from Melbourne.

This was also the period of ideological literary journals, three of which flourished or were born in the 1950s. It was an ideological decade, even if many poets declined to acknowledge it. But poetry, while it was affected, was not determined by ideological conflict. The decade was dominated by those who had begun to exert creative force in the previous decade, and new poets were seen as joining a living line. For example, while the remarkable Randolph Stow published his first book of poetry, *Act One*, in 1957, Slessor's *Poems* and a volume by Wright appeared in the same year. The Thompson, Slessor, Howarth Penguin anthology appeared the next year; and then Fitzgerald and Hart-Smith published volumes of verse, McAuley and Wright volumes of prose; and Hope and Stewart reappeared. The only weakening in the established pattern was that poets were no longer disposed to see the nature-lyricism of Douglas Stewart and his allies as itself natural. Its hold on Australian poetry had been weakened by Slessor's long silence and Kenneth Mackenzie's untimely death; and the *Bulletin*, their oldest centre, was shortly to change hands not long before their other resource, the publishing house of Angus and Robertson.

Other changes had occurred. The nurturing institution to which poetry attached itself was no longer publishing or journalism but universities and colleges. While the full implications of this are hard to state, they do not necessarily mean that poetry was or is now in the hands of academics: they may mean diversification, a chance for pluralism. But it was then, by the logic of linked mistakes, that the long quarrel arose between poets and academics, which developed into a quarrel between 'academic' and other poets. The ludicrous terms of this discussion were replicated, as James McAuley pointed out, in the public service, where after the war the 'practical men' resented their juniors getting university degrees.

As later decades show, it is not possible to set up so clear an opposition between two syndromes. All Australian poets are disadvantaged by the same comparative neglect. They are all, except for a favoured few, disadvantaged by the international system of publication and distribution. They read poets who will never get the chance to read them. These include many poets who are read in translation, some of whom have been translated by Australians. There is also an increasing awareness of New Zealand poetry, and growing contacts with Canada, Scotland and Ireland.

How could anyone regret such pluralism, such openness, which England and America also enjoy? Given it, we can no longer speak of a national poetry, if indeed we ever could. Australian poetry did not develop in isolation; it was always part of a network, and the puzzle that afflicted it was to know what part the network assigned it. There were models even for its nationalism, and affiliates for its nativism. All Australian poets read the poetry of other civilizations; in that respect they were like their English counterparts. As distances melt, it is quite clear that you cannot shape a country's poetry as if you were making butter; even if you know where the cream comes from, you can never be sure of the salt. All individuals will provide for themselves, and those who can't get what they need will make do with what they can.

But what disappears as an issue may linger as a habit, and the old splits may return as a subtext to a seemingly harmonized art. The Australian habit of deference is so deep-rooted that deference is paid liberally to English poets, to French and German, to Japanese and Indonesian, and above all to North American. Australian agencies have been known to pay for visits to foreign poets and also to be visited by them. These prized reference-groups have also provided poetic models, the more easily in some cases since their poetry is distributed in Australia without a reciprocal arrangement –

thus continuing in an exotic form that most bizarre of economic systems, unilateral free trade.

The question, then, is not one of isolation but one of pressure. Has Australian poetry been under pressure to conform to something it did not feel growing inside it? For most of its life it *was* under pressure, internally through the whole education system, and externally through its colonial position, which placed it in the shadow of other poetries. It has survived these pressures without retreating towards isolationism. By 1960, as Thomas Shapcott puts it, we had a 'detailed critique of intellectual responsibility' which prevented such a retreat. So, of course, did the great sweeps of post-war migration, which naturally brought with them poets, potential poets, and bodies of poetry in more than a hundred languages. Although circumstances keep me to poetry written in English, I am aware that Australian poetry is not just poetry written by Anglophone Australians. Poets who write in Italian, Greek, Spanish or Arabic bring with them the possibilities for our poetry of the poetries on which their work relies. But this process is young, and I have little better than cliché to indicate its nature. What *can* be said is that it finishes isolationism.

The 1960s are seen by some poets as the time when modern poetry – or quite simply, poetry – came at last to Australia. They would reject not just one orthodoxy but all: Hope as well as Fitzgerald, Wright as well as Dawe; and they would see national self-realization in the great proliferation of forms and poetries which came here in the late 1960s from all quarters at once, especially from America the golden. These claims are made by people who frequently reject one another as well as their elders. Certainly, the American influence began to be solicited very urgently and in the end systematically by editors who wanted to infuse our poetry with energies they had felt themselves. Thomas Shapcott was the chief of these poets, and in the role of editor he gained more overseas contact than anyone before him. In doing so, he and others were implicitly challenging the older poets, from all groups, to show that their poetry could face up to the important stimulus of language and form which America provided. For a time there was a united avant-garde; but Shapcott was soon attacked by those he had sponsored.

In any case he did not invent the American connection. Many Australian poets, especially the Melbourne ones, had been stimulated by a variety of American poets from the mid-1940s, the very time when the *annus mirabilis* produced renewal from within.

At the beginning of the 1960s, when a new consciousness was leading poets abroad, Francis Webb came home from an expatriation of almost a decade, from psychiatric hospitals in England to others in Australia. He became a focus of meaning, a creative example, for poets like Beaver and Robert Adamson, who saw him as *il miglior fabbro*, and saw the persistence of his art as a stimulus and challenge to them. Bruce Dawe* was back too, for most of the decade, writing those abundant poems which made him in some ways the quintessential Australian poet. From the first he formalized in verse an accent and intonation which existed everywhere in Australia: a demotic accent and a sardonic intonation, in which he reported ironically on one injustice after another, making central a new form of the open conscience.

The Cold War in its old form had disappeared, and political antagonisms were of little account. There was a great surge of political consciousness, however, coming from protests against the Indo-Chinese wars, to which Australian troops were committed. Most poets who expressed a view were against this commitment; nobody published pro-war poems. Beaver and Dawe were the most powerful voices, and no one could mistake how exactly their feelings about that human crisis fitted their feelings about language. Protest was inevitable for them: protest, outcry, and lament. Consciousness of the war was everywhere, implicating all the issues of authority and social cohesion that such wars release for debate.

Oddly, perhaps, the widespread changes in consciousness were accompanied not only by greater empathy with American poets and poetry, but also by a growth in nationalist

*The selection of Dawe's work in this anthology is limited to six poems by Dawe's own rule. – P.B.

feeling. This took different forms, but did not lead to the earlier bitterly divisive insistence that national caring demanded nationalist attitudes, subject-matter, even national poetic forms. Pluralism could not be expunged now.

It seems to me that the 1960s were remarkable not for the indiscriminate replication of overseas influences but for the growth of such important poets as Harwood, Beaver and Dawe. Although two of them were influenced by America, all three were distinguished by a deep and passionate individuality; they were not operating on the basis of any consensus such as had been common from the 1920s onward. The 1960s were the time of individual accomplishment, and the shedding, without fuss, of aesthetic consensualism.

1969 was the year in which *Letters to Live Poets* appeared, the finest book by Bruce Beaver, who developed remarkably in this decade. It was also one of the years of supposed revolution as sponsored by John Tranter at the time, and recorded by him ten years later in *The New Australian Poetry*. In so far as this was anti-humanist, it gave a new dimension to our poetry, and a new issue for debate. But the contending parties rarely went as far as debate; chiefly they *edited* at each other. For this, it was necessary to have control of journals, and if possible of publishing programmes. Tranter and some of his friends had several small magazines, of which only *New Poetry* was very substantial. And they confronted another group even more entrenched than they, which centred on Les A. Murray and which included Geoffrey Lehmann, Geoff Page and Mark O'Connor, although the most talented poet after Murray was undoubtedly Robert Gray.

Tranter's anthology includes Beaver, but in general it resolutely excludes older poets. It would be fair to say that Murray's field of influence does likewise; it may invoke certain older poets, but it does not promote them. The struggle is between two groups of the one generation.

The Tranter anthology introduces, chiefly, a new pressure, a new sense of power. The anthology which responds to it, edited by Lehmann and Gray, has the dullness of its correctness. This is often the case when poets insist on being a group and exerting pressure. Such tribal reactions are a pity. The claim that a body of poetry is or has been inadequate to the times can always be tested, and the discussion can quickly lead to questions about the very core of the country's life. Australians are shy of prolonged debate, so much less stylish than assertion; and they may be correct in thinking that power and standing can be secured much more surely by organizational means. Say nothing, and outflank 'em.

So what it is about is hard for the outsider to say, and perhaps a patient and sceptical gaze is the one to cultivate. There are elements of the old debate between internationalism and nativism, but these do not take us very far; everyone is now in an international network of influence. The Search for a National Identity is an empty cliché for the emptiest of symposia, and it is generally realized that one poet's identity is another's anomie, one's coming of age may well drive another into the cycles of regression. The field is open for whatever experiments can be conducted.

Until fairly recently, British and Irish poetry have been less influential than one might have expected, given that they have been widely read; while the American influence has been heavy and various. Even some who are often regarded as members of a nativist counter-movement are in this position; Robert Gray, for example, has Australianized William Carlos Williams to splendid effect. But this general influence, so strong in recent decades, no longer has much overt power with substantial poets. It is possible that, wearied by gestures that indicate more than they can deliver, some poets are developing in step with recent English poetry; and Peter Porter is probably the vital link.

The decline of debates coincides with greater diversity of talents. Perhaps, even so, a hidden consensus has persisted, or has returned, a silent majority telling us what people really want to write and to read. If so, it is still rural, not urban, in location. In all the reading I have done in recent years, I have been struck by the percentage of good poems which are located outside cities, in open habitats ranging from hills to deserts. The urbanization of our poetry, so long awaited and so rightly desired, has not proved as resonant as the hinterlands. This has surprised me, and so has the extent to which this open quality (something too positive and primitive to be called pastoral) goes with pictures of earlier generations suffering their adaptation; it is ancestral, a generational wonder and piety, a concern for parents and grandparents as examples and victims. The motif is usually loneliness, and the word processors are resonating with the myths of the Nineties, but it is all tied to the sense of being nurtured, and of nurturing the land. The verbal experience of Australians is largely a country one.

There are other changes which are really continuities. Discovery has been supplanted as a subject by the First World War, and especially by Gallipoli, in which the nation was thought to have matured, come of age, and had its baptism of fire. A deep degree of piety, with the attendant pity, has gone into themes of Gallipoli, so that something of a tissue of debate has been woven about it, by Wallace-Crabbe, Page, Murray, John Forbes and others. There may be militarist interests in some of this, but I think that generally the poets are fascinated by the otherness of something very close to them, which has made a fault-line in their family histories. Similarly, the stories of exploration (of others travelling to find a source for all) have been supplanted by stories of one's own mobility: travelling on the interstate highways, hitching from one disorientating hamlet to another, leaving or going home over great distances, going abroad, reporting from Asia or Europe or the Barrier Reef, finding facets of oneself in America, losing one's stereotype in Greece. All of this has enlarged the store of experiences, motifs and plaints, though in ways which owe more to North Americans and their automobile-fetishism than, say, to myths of original journeying, Ulysses or Aeneas or Moses or St Brendan. Even so, the travelling has activated myths which must have lain prepotent in the imagination.

One reason why Australia has had no single, definite, central tradition of poetry in this century is that it has had no dominant central poet. Slessor was the nearest thing to such a central figure in the early modern period, but his influence is much smaller than the respect which he is finally given. There has been no poet whose performance, ideology, sins and unpredictability govern talk at conferences and in journals.

No one fills the role of Wallace Stevens in Ivy League land or William Carlos Williams in Urban County; no one has the magnetizing power of Eliot. At any given time four or five poets have been writing with roughly equal status.

It is only recently that an exception has arisen, as Les A. Murray has come to be seen by more and more people as the most energetic figure in our present poetry, and in some sense its centre. It is interesting that this view of him is taken by classroom teachers more often than by his fellow poets, although some of these would no doubt agree. And it is interesting that his gaining such stature back home should coincide with his gaining it abroad, in New York, London and Edinburgh. More people talk about Murray than about any other Australian poet. Why is this? Because he radiates power, certainty and conviction at the same time as he shows versatility, virtuoso abilities and a quite unusual inventiveness. He is also felt to be in touch with the most primaeval forces of the country, enjoying in this respect a reputation something like Ted Hughes or Seamus Heaney. He is Earthman, assured of the Earth-Spirit.

Murray has reached pre-eminence at the point where the *academic* study of Australian poetry has become widespread and conventional. This is no accident: Murray is a natural food for the seminar, because he is a discursive poet, and because he discourses in his own way on many things which arouse controversy. Whether or not they agree with him, people are happy to discuss him. Yet there is a paradox in the academy's taking to its bosom so assertive a spokesman of anti-academic values.

He can be strikingly direct and simple, as in the opening of his 'Immigrant Voyage', the most eloquent poem I know about the post-war migrations:

> My wife came out on the *Goya*
> in the mid-year of our century.
>
> In the fogs of that winter
> many hundred ships were sounding;
> the DP camps were being washed to sea . . .

> Hull-down and pouring light
> the tithe-barns, the cathedrals
> were bearing the old castes away.

But he has developed a more and more rococo form, a longer-breathed rhetoric, to oppose his 'laconics', and it would be idle to speculate whether he will convert or transcend this garrulity and become the great poet whose latency has so often been signalled.

The other poet who dominated the 1970s was Bruce Beaver, a poet very unlike Murray, who shared with him nevertheless an ease with the long line and paragraph and a pronounced lyric surface. Beaver's strength lies in his contemplative intelligence and his deeply musical instinct. After *Letters to Live Poets* (1969), which was a sequence of diversified but often passionate reflections, he came to specialize in 'sets'; subsequent volumes set a collection of Lauds against one of Plaints, and produced sets of Odes to put against Days. This imaginative formula, which relies so much on ancient traditions, worked very well for Beaver, as did his wide-ranging poems in *Death's Directives*.

Two or three other poets have been central to our poetry for forty years. As Murray has grown more elaborate and Beaver more daring, Judith Wright may have seemed to go on an even keel, neither stirring up the depths nor striking out for far waters. In the middle of her journey, in the 1960s, she was rather taken for granted; and more recently she has sometimes been spoken of as someone who had given up poetry for ecological activism. Even so, rather than declining, the respect in which she was held has grown; and of course her prose works, which are very distinguished, increased her charisma. Reading the *oeuvre* as a whole makes it clear how consistently she has followed her life's task; her poetry is driven by some subliminal tide of passion, whose note has deepened with the years, taking her to more fundamental realizations of what had always been her concern: the relations of women to men, for example, or of women to women; or femaleness as such. One might say that she has gone so far without anyone's noticing because most of her work, from first to last, has been done in neat, shapely forms with a general air of seemliness coming through the eloquence. In some ways, the same road has been followed by Gwen Harwood, who has come in her latest works to most fundamental things, as mother to still-born child, or daughter to mother. Her passion is ardent, immediate and dominant, and perhaps it is that which has kept her outside poetic groupings and debates about mod-ernism, practising an art which comes from an inner life fed by non-polemical sources, as disinterested as the music she loves.

The other poet about whom something should be said is A. D. Hope, with Fitzgerald's death the senior poet of the country. He has recently published a substantial volume, and continues with inimitable zest his personal campaign against modernism. It is not clear that anyone agrees with his reasoning, and his influence is as an example rather than a model; for no one tries to write like him. Yet admirers, particularly of his earlier poetry, come from many quarters. That poetry showed an absolutism which still exists, though in softened forms. Characteristically, he still goes in for addition and elaboration, and is a narrative poet, as far from imagist compression as one can imagine; but joking has replaced satire. He is an example of the artist who has had his effect and is admired because of his atypicality.

The generation succeeding his has recently lost many of its members by death: McAuley, Campbell, Manifold, Stewart. Except in the case of Campbell, the loss was not of innovative power, but of achieved style. Following Slessor, several poets of that generation developed an interest in bearing which conveyed an element of linguistic dandyism; yet they were serious and inspiriting examples. The stylishness may be one of the legacies they accepted from Yeats, and perhaps Auden, for they were the first generation to be exposed radically to the mature influence of those poets. Although all of them had a lively connection with overseas poetries, they show very little of the American influence which was to become dominant twenty years after they had entered the scene.

The 1970s, which saw the deaths of several of these poets, also produced habits of which they would probably have disapproved. For example, there was and is still a taste for sequences, and, because many people seemed to find it hard to delineate a subject, for stream-of-association poetry. Some poets also resorted to sets, as in the sonnets by Tranter, Scott and others, and sets of more sophisticated conception, like Beaver's. All this barely preceded the turning by several poets to the novel: it was a good time for it, when 'novels' could be 'post-modernist' structures rather like long poems conducted at a different rhythm. Malouf and Roger McDonald have taken to prose fiction with something like the finality which Stow showed much earlier. Shapcott may also be heading in that direction. Murray wrote his 'novel' in verse – in sonnets, indeed – and promptly went back to more convenient patterns. But we must suppose this trend will continue, and will weaken the influence of the middle generation on younger poets. John Scott embeds short passages of poetry in stretches of prose. Laurie Duggan's recent work on the settlement of Gippsland uses novelistic techniques in a verse influenced by Snyder and Dorn. The novelizing of our poetry is under way.

It is hard to estimate the 1970s as a unit, to analyse a terrain so close at hand and so variously populated. I have an impression of undefined conflicts, of bodies of poetry written in languages other than English, not yet clearly visible in the context of Anglophone poetry, of translations from Aboriginal languages putting other poetry to shame by the depth and delicacy of their carnal knowledge of the land, and of networks of contacts deliberately and intelligently established with other countries throughout the world. Poets who teach in universities and colleges have been useful here, by using their leave periods partly for this purpose. The main agency is of course the Literature Board of the Arts Council. The contacts made now will probably create influences for the next two or three decades.

*

The editorial principles I have followed are governed by circumstances as well as convictions about what an anthology of this size should and should not try to do. Not everyone will agree with all of them, and some of them may seem designed to exclude. They are in fact designed to highlight the distinctive and developing strengths of Australian poetry in a given period. To achieve this I have had to leave out poets, poems, and kinds of poem which might belong richly to another anthology.

As I read through the scores of books and hundreds of journals, two convictions grew in me: that there is far more poetry worthy to be made permanent than one can get into any anthology, written by more poets than one might have expected; and that if the group of important poets is far superior to the rest, it is not because they have written great poems but because they have written so many good ones. This is true of Slessor, Hope, Wright, Webb, Harwood; but in some of those cases it is concealed by the popularity of a few anthology pieces. The economy at which I arrived starts with the obvious: to re-present the big largely.

Its corollary is: do not assume that bigness can be achieved by association, by apparent membership of a group – each claim must be scrutinized separately. This will lead to annoyance; it is common in Australia for commentators not to stop at naming one poet or two, but to name several members of one generation, who thus become the aristocracy for that generation. Leonie Kramer has done this with the generation of Wright and McAuley. But it is easy for groups of associates to turn into interest-groups. Now there are more groups than ever, some based on ideology, some on religion, some on propinquity, some on technique, and some on mere habit. One has to try to ignore or circumvent all such arrangements. Propinquity, of course, is stronger than ideology, and habit harder to resist than power.

For obvious reasons, it has to be a short-poems anthology. The maximum length was set for me by Slessor's 'Five Bells', and Fitzgerald's 'The Wind at Your Door', which forced me to exclude Hope's 'The Double Looking Glass'. On a similar principle, I have left out poems which seemed too long for their content or their rhythm, poems in which the theme or rhythm seemed exhausted before they ended; some poets who habitually write in this accumulative way have not been included.

Some poets, too (Jennifer Maiden, Rodney Hall and Thomas Shapcott are examples), seem to produce a continuum of poetry rather than a collection of distinct works. There is as great a fashion for the undeclared sequence as there is for the declared one. Representing such poetry in an anthology leads to an effect of sampling rather than of highlighting. I do not wish to create this effect, and I have found no way of representing most of these poets while avoiding it.

For similar reasons, avowed sequences of considerable length have been excluded. Many of these are in fact long poems. I have included some examples of poems taken from sequences in which the sections are in fact separate poems.

I have overlooked 'concrete' poems, prose poems, and translations from foreign languages. This rule is hard on such poets as Philip Martin, whose best quality seems to me to have come out in his translations. It also creates difficulties in representing such a poet as Dimitris Tsaloumas, who has published poems in English and in Greek, and translations by himself as well as by others. I have considered only his poems in English and his own translations from the Greek, but the fewness of these does not enable him to be represented fully.

The hidden text in my brief was 'What came to happen in Australian poetry from 1920 onwards?'; and so I excluded those poets who, although they lived and often published beyond 1920, seemed clearly to belong to another time and to genres on the edge of extinction. They included Baylebridge, Brennan, Mary Gilmore (who wrote for decades within our period), and my greatest regret, Banjo Paterson, whose finest poems also need a lot of space. Hugh McCrae might also have been excluded on such grounds, I suppose, but my actual reason was that I think him not nearly as good as many critics do, or did. Shaw Neilson is my deliberate exception to this rule, because his poems seem to me in some way free of time-bonds. This is a common perception of him among Australians.

The problem as I put it to myself was not how to exclude but on what basis to include. My strong preference is for representing a poet by at least three poems, and I have managed this in most cases; tokenism of various sorts has ruined many anthologies while pleasing many poets. I regret many of the exclusions necessitated by this principle; there are so many poets who have a case for inclusion, and I have hesitated over all of them. Quarrels about them have no outcome, and are not worth anticipating.

When I look at the final ensemble, I suspect there are too many rather than too few names, and too many reasonably good poets represented too sparsely. I have gone in every case for what I thought had vitality, life in the rhythm and language, and have seldom been impressed by the kinds of scenario-setting which are the academic verse of the present day.

Ern Malley, the invented poet who became a legendary voice, and who, whether or not he existed, uttered some memorable passages, I decided to leave out only because space is so limited.

I have not taken up the question of 'the vernacular', which is more difficult to isolate than is often thought, and easily becomes a false question. Its opposite, mandarin poetry, seems not to produce rhythmically interesting verse, and there is not much of it around. In effect the whole collection might be called vernacular, for it is written in verse adaptations of various kinds of Australian speech patterns. There is no one Australian vernacular, but a shifting pattern of vernacular usages which, for a brief time, settle to present one vernacular or another. No important poet uses stage-Aussie except for occasional, usually mocking, effect. My own opinion is that questions of 'identity' and of national distinctiveness in the language should not be whipped up to keep each other running; poetry gains in no way from such excitement.

Some vernacular intonations are unfortunately not represented, however. There are no ballads, and few poems I should call 'work poems'. Good poems about work and sport are rare. Nor are there representations of Anglophone Aboriginal poets, such as Kevin Gilbert, Bobbi Sykes and Jack Davis. Gilbert's work is particularly memorable to me, but his book *People Are Legends* works to an unusual degree by internal reinforcement: the poems support one another by echo and parallel. In isolation, they lack resonance.

I did not look for 'Australianness' of reference or manner; there was no need to do so, and I should not have known how to begin. In any case, it is rarely that one hears 'essential Australianness' being claimed for an Australian poet in the way one hears of the 'essential Englishness' of Larkin or Geoffrey Hill, and no doubt many another. Such concepts come and go with the ideological weather. There is less than I wanted of poetry that answers to Milton's 'simple, sensuous and passionate'; such poetry seems at a discount in all Anglophone countries.

I am not in a position to consider the influence of the women's movement on our poetry, although I think it must be large. What is clear is that poetry by women became much stronger in the 1940s and 1950s than it had been before, and that it has continued to strengthen phase by phase up till the present, in a way that may have something to do with the fine late development in the work of Wright, Harwood and Elizabeth Riddell, and the dramatic changes in the style of Dorothy Hewett.

In some cases I have tried to show the diversity in a poet's work, although in a case such as that of Hope the very expansiveness of his poems defeated me. In other cases (Rhyll McMaster, Robert Adamson and Evan Jones are examples) I have concentrated on poems of one kind, or from one period, in order to show their chief strength in a small space.

Expatriates are not penalized, but each case has to be considered on its own terms: most of Randolph Stow's poems, for example, were written in Australia or are located here, while Peter Porter raises a quite different problem. I have taken the view that, as an Australian-born poet who has over recent years repeatedly visited Australia and concerned himself with its poetry, he should be represented, and in no merely token way; but that it is idle to pretend that his work is not part of English poetry, and that it should be represented on the same basis as that of Webb or Beaver. It is tempting to print work in which he states a view of Australia, as he does in several late poems; but these are not among his finest, and I think he is at his best when he writes in the context of the England in which he lives. I have made my selection on those grounds.

It has been hardest to resist temptation in the matter of works from the Aboriginal languages. These would have to be translations, and many translations already exist, some of them published in recent anthologies. They are generally reprinted from scholarly journals. It is hard to know what principles should be given priority, for when one asks of *what* they are translations, the answer is that they are translations of part of an Aboriginal art-work, but not of the whole; the poems are the verbal components of ceremonial actions, which usually also involve dancing and music, and perhaps some additional forms of drama. When printed in translation, they exist in a world irrevocably foreign and perhaps inimical to them. Further, the translations are of something transcribed, usually by European scholars, not by Aboriginal artists themselves. I cannot bring myself to believe that I have the right to declare these translations either Aboriginal or poems; they may of course be both in other minds.

It is lack of space, rather than over-niceness, that persuaded me not to seek out 'popular poetry' of the sorts which produced such splendid songs and ballads in the first century or more of white settlement. Merely to sample these works is pointless. Whether they flourish now as they did some decades ago I simply do not know; I suspect not; but even if they did I could print only a token few. Nor have I tried to convert street poetry, or performance poetry, to printed form; they have chosen their medium, and voices are not printable any more than ceremonial dances are.

The terminal date for this anthology is 1980. I have chosen no poem known to have been written after that date except (in a few cases) to supplement and illuminate earlier poems by an author.

Given these decisions, the volume will have a preponderance of fairly brief, firmly shaped poems which aim at a concentration of lyrical or other statement. It is my belief that the strongest tendency in Australian poetry runs towards poems of lyric scope. At times the poetry has shown an almost fetishistic concern with neatness, firmness of shape, clear or wry endings; yet, paradoxically, freedom has been achieved in poems which, transcending their aspect ot neatness, have turned glib closure into cadence. The other dominant Australian tendency, towards over-elaboration, will naturally not be found very often in these pages.

The criteria of selection are in the end deeply subjective ones, and their application has had to rely to an extent on guesswork. I have asked myself openly: Are these poems memorable, and will they last? The finest anthologists have followed the principle dictated by these questions – some, like Yeats, with an eccentric tilt towards the memorable, some with a strong instinct for durability, as with Matthiessen and Vincent O'Sullivan. These two concerns seem to me to be joined in another, which demands a further question, precisely that of economy: Does this shape, this music, this deep form have an equivalence with this Saying? Such a question suits short poems, and hence the poems in this collection. Will this poem or that, asks the collector, still be alive in twenty years? If so, it will be because it says as much as it sings. From that point of view, I am confident of the poems here.

V.B.

Publisher's Note

The selection of Vincent Buckley's verse contained in this anthology was made by Penelope Buckley and Chris Wallace-Crabbe.

John Shaw Neilson (1872–1942)

The Orange Tree

The young girl stood beside me. I
   Saw not what her young eyes could see:
– A light, she said, not of the sky
   Lives somewhere in the Orange Tree.

– Is it, I said, of east or west?
   The heartbeat of a luminous boy
Who with his faltering flute confessed
   Only the edges of his joy?

Was he, I said, borne to the blue
   In a mad escapade of Spring
Ere he could make a fond adieu
   To his love in the blossoming?

– Listen! the young girl said. There calls
   No voice, no music beats on me;
But it is almost sound: it falls
   This evening on the Orange Tree.

– Does he, I said, so fear the Spring
   Ere the white sap too far can climb?
See in the full gold evening
   All happenings of the olden time?

Is he so goaded by the green?
   Does the compulsion of the dew
Make him unknowable but keen
   Asking with beauty of the blue?

– Listen! the young girl said. For all
   Your hapless talk you fail to see
There is a light, a step, a call
   This evening on the Orange Tree.

– Is it, I said, a waste of love
   Imperishably old in pain,
Moving as an affrighted dove
   Under the sunlight or the rain?

Is it a fluttering heart that gave
   Too willingly and was reviled?
Is it the stammering at a grave,
   The last word of a little child?

– Silence! the young girl said. Oh, why,
   Why will you talk to weary me?
Plague me no longer now, for I
   Am listening like the Orange Tree.

Colour Yourself for a Man

The seers may chasten; the fools may bid the waters dance
   uphill;
The seers may sorrow that little of all in the world can heed
   their will:
The hills may fall to the vales, and earth forget where the
   rivers ran:
Listen, Sally! Stifle your woes: colour your eyes and lips and
   hose!
      Colour yourself for a man!

Thirst is Heaven, and thirst is Hell, and every fire between;
And Famine is old as the Winter time, and Pain is an
   evergreen:
Thirst is the maker of thieves; so, take every colour you can!
– Every glitter about the day; colour your words on the
   tiresome way!
      Colour yourself for a man!

[2]

Colour is life and hate and heat and a million joys beside:
'Tis vanity keeps the world awake, and the wealth in a man
   is pride:
Thirst is the mother of theft, and theft was old when the
   world began:
Listen, Sally! Stifle your woes: colour your thoughts and
   eyes and hose!
       Colour yourself for a man!

The Sun Is Up

Speak not of Death: it is a merry morn;
A glittering bird has danced into a tree:
From his abundant heart bravely are born
The loves of leafy choristers to me:
Music is of the sunlight, strong and free . . .
The sun is up, and Death is far away:
The first hour is the sweetest of the day.

Blithely a bush boy wanders on a walk –
Shaking with joy, joyous in heart and limb:
For his delight the trees have learned to talk
And all the flowers have little laughs with him
Watching the far sky, wonderful and dim . . .
The sun is up, and Death is far away:
The first hour is the sweetest of the day.

Stony Town

If I ever go to Stony Town, I'll go as to a fair,
With bells and men and a dance-girl with the heat-wave in
    her hair:
I'll ask the birds that live on the road; for I dream (though it
    may not be)
That the eldest song was a forest thought and the singer
    was a tree.

Oh, Stony Town is a hard town! It buys and sells and buys:
It will not pity the plights of youth or any love in the eyes:
No curve they follow in Stony Town; but the straight line
    and the square:
– And the girl shall dance them a royal dance, like a blue
    wren at his prayer.

Oh, Stony Town is a hard town! It sells and buys and sells:
– Merry men three I will take with me, and seven and
    twenty bells:
The bells will laugh and the men will laugh, and the girl
    shall shine so fair
With the scent of love and cinnamon dust shaken out of her
    hair.

Her skirts shall be of the gossamer, full thirty inches high;
And her lips shall move as the flowers move to see the
    winds go by:
The men will laugh, and the bells will laugh, to find the
    world so young;
And the girl shall go as a velvet bird, with a quick step on
    her tongue.

[4]

She shall cry aloud that a million moons for a lover is not
  long,
And her mouth shall be as the green honey in the honey-
  eater's song:
– If ever I go to Stony Town, I'll go as to a fair,
And the girl shall shake with the cinnamon and the heat-
  wave in her hair.

Take Down the Fiddle, Karl!

Men openly call you the enemy, call you the swine,
But all that they say to me never can make you a foeman of
  mine.
The rain has come over the mountains, the gullies have
  faded away;
Take down the fiddle, Karl! the little old impudent fiddle:
  the work is all done for the day.

The ganger sits down in the bar-room with money to spend,
And many will laugh at his loudness, and many will hail
  him as friend.
How strong the mist settles! it sinks in the souls of us all.
Take down the fiddle, Karl! the little old impudent fiddle
  that hangs on the peg on the wall.

We are tired of the jack-hammers' clatter, the rattle of stone,
The many who boast of their travels, the many who moan;
We are tired of the spoil and the spoilers, the lifting of clay:
Take down the fiddle, Karl! the little old impudent fiddle:
  the work is all over today.

Your fiddle will show me your fathers, the hunt of the boar;
How dark were the forests! but fairies were seen at the
door;
And in the old chapel your fathers bareheaded they came in
to pray:
Take down the fiddle, Karl! the little old impudent fiddle:
the work is all over today.

The fiddle is old but the things it is saying will ever be
young;
It goes out and tries to be saying what cannot be sung.
The speech that you have, Karl, to me it means nothing at
all:
Take down the fiddle, Karl! the little old impudent fiddle
that hangs on the peg on the wall.

The fiddle can give us no more than the drinking of wine;
It brings up a world of good fellows to your eyes and mine.
The ganger, poor man, is misguided, his world is so grey:
Take down the fiddle, Karl! the little old impudent fiddle:
the work is all done for the day.

Kenneth Slessor (1901–71)

The Night-Ride

Gas flaring on the yellow platform; voices running up and
    down;
Milk-tins in cold dented silver; half-awake I stare,
Pull up the blind, blink out – all sounds are drugged;
The slow blowing of passengers asleep;
Engines yawning; water in heavy drips;
Black, sinister travellers, lumbering up the station,
One moment in the window, hooked over bags;
Hurrying, unknown faces – boxes with strange labels –
All groping clumsily to mysterious ends,
Out of the gaslight, dragged by private Fates.
Their echoes die. The dark train shakes and plunges;
Bells cry out; the night-ride starts again.
Soon I shall look out into nothing but blackness,
Pale, windy fields. The old roar and knock of the rails
Melts in dull fury. Pull down the blind. Sleep. Sleep.
Nothing but grey, rushing rivers of bush outside.
Gaslight and milk-cans. Of Rapptown I recall nothing else.

Wild Grapes

The old orchard, full of smoking air,
Full of sour marsh and broken boughs, is there,
But kept no more by vanished Mulligans,
Or Hartigans, long drowned in earth themselves,
Who gave this bitter fruit their care.

Here's where the cherries grew that birds forgot,
And apples bright as dogstars; now there is not
An apple or a cherry; only grapes,
But wild ones, Isabella grapes they're called,
Small, pointed, black, like boughs of musket-shot.

[7]

Eating their flesh, half-savage with black fur,
Acid and gipsy-sweet, I thought of her,
Isabella, the dead girl, who has lingered on
Defiantly when all have gone away,
In an old orchard where swallows never stir.

Isabella grapes, outlaws of a strange bough,
That in their harsh sweetness remind me somehow
Of dark hair swinging and silver pins,
A girl half-fierce, half-melting, as these grapes,
Kissed here – or killed here – but who remembers now?

Talbingo

'Talbingo River' – as one says of bones:
'Captain' or 'Commodore' that smelt gunpowder
In old engagements no one quite believes
Or understands. Talbingo had its blood
As they did, ran with waters huge and clear
Lopping down mountains,
Turning crags to banks.

Now it's a sort of aching valley,
Basalt shaggy with scales,
A funnel of tobacco-coloured clay,
Smoulders of puffed earth
And pebbles and shell-bodied flies
And water thickening to stone in pocks.

That's what we're like out here,
Beds of dried-up passions.

Country Towns

Country towns, with your willows and squares,
And farmers bouncing on barrel mares
To public-houses of yellow wood
With '1860' over their doors,
And that mysterious race of Hogans
Which always keeps General Stores . . .

At the School of Arts, a broadsheet lies
Sprayed with the sarcasm of flies:
'The Great Golightly Family
Of Entertainers Here To-night' –
Dated a year and a half ago,
But left there, less from carelessness
Than from a wish to seem polite.

Verandas baked with musky sleep,
Mulberry faces dozing deep,
And dogs that lick the sunlight up
Like paste of gold – or, roused in vain
By far, mysterious buggy-wheels,
Lower their ears, and drowse again . . .

Country towns with your schooner bees,
And locusts burnt in the pepper-trees,
Drown me with syrups, arch your boughs,
Find me a bench, and let me snore,
Till, charged with ale and unconcern,
I'll think it's noon at half-past four!

North Country

North Country, filled with gesturing wood,
With trees that fence, like archers' volleys,
The flanks of hidden valleys
Where nothing's left to hide

But verticals and perpendiculars,
Like rain gone wooden, fixed in falling,
Or fingers blindly feeling
For what nobody cares;

Or trunks of pewter, bangled by greedy death,
Stuck with black staghorns, quietly sucking,
And trees whose boughs go seeking,
And trees like broken teeth

With smoky antlers broken in the sky;
Or trunks that lie grotesquely rigid,
Like bodies blank and wretched
After a fool's battue,

As if they've secret ways of dying here
And secret places for their anguish
When boughs at last relinquish
Their clench of blowing air –

But this gaunt country, filled with mills and saws,
With butter-works and railway-stations
And public institutions,
And scornful rumps of cows,

North Country, filled with gesturing wood –
Timber's the end it gives to branches,
Cut off in cubic inches,
Dripping red with blood.

South Country

After the whey-faced anonymity
Of river-gums and scribbly-gums and bush,
After the rubbing and the hit of brush,
You come to the South Country

As if the argument of trees were done,
The doubts and quarrelling, the plots and pains,
All ended by these clear and gliding planes
Like an abrupt solution.

And over the flat earth of empty farms
The monstrous continent of air floats back
Coloured with rotting sunlight and the black,
Bruised flesh of thunderstorms:

Air arched, enormous, pounding the bony ridge,
Ditches and hutches, with a drench of light,
So huge, from such infinities of height,
You walk on the sky's beach

While even the dwindled hills are small and bare,
As if, rebellious, buried, pitiful,
Something below pushed up a knob of skull,
Feeling its way to air.

Five Bells

Time that is moved by little fidget wheels
Is not my Time, the flood that does not flow.
Between the double and the single bell
Of a ship's hour, between a round of bells
From the dark warship riding there below,
I have lived many lives, and this one life
Of Joe, long dead, who lives between five bells.

Deep and dissolving verticals of light
Ferry the falls of moonshine down. Five bells
Coldly rung out in a machine's voice. Night and water
Pour to one rip of darkness, the Harbour floats
In air, the Cross hangs upside-down in water.

Why do I think of you, dead man, why thieve
These profitless lodgings from the flukes of thought
Anchored in Time? You have gone from earth,
Gone even from the meaning of a name;
Yet something's there, yet something forms its lips
And hits and cries against the ports of space,
Beating their sides to make its fury heard.

Are you shouting at me, dead man, squeezing your face
In agonies of speech on speechless panes?
Cry louder, beat the windows, bawl your name!

But I hear nothing, nothing . . . only bells,
Five bells, the bumpkin calculus of Time.
Your echoes die, your voice is dowsed by Life,
There's not a mouth can fly the pygmy strait –
Nothing except the memory of some bones
Long shoved away, and sucked away, in mud;
And unimportant things you might have done,
Or once I thought you did; but you forgot,
And all have now forgotten – looks and words
And slops of beer; your coat with buttons off,
Your gaunt chin and pricked eye, and raging tales
Of Irish kings and English perfidy,
And dirtier perfidy of publicans
Groaning to God from Darlinghurst.

Five bells.

Then I saw the road, I heard the thunder
Tumble, and felt the talons of the rain
The night we came to Moorebank in slab-dark,
So dark you bore no body, had no face,
But a sheer voice that rattled out of air
(As now you'd cry if I could break the glass),
A voice that spoke beside me in the bush,
Loud for a breath or bitten off by wind,
Of Milton, melons, and the Rights of Man,
And blowing flutes, and how Tahitian girls
Are brown and angry-tongued, and Sydney girls

Are white and angry-tongued, or so you'd found.
But all I heard was words that didn't join
So Milton became melons, melons girls,
And fifty mouths, it seemed, were out that night,
And in each tree an Ear was bending down,
Or something had just run, gone behind grass,
When, blank and bone-white, like a maniac's thought,
The naphtha-flash of lightning slit the sky,
Knifing the dark with deathly photographs.
There's not so many with so poor a purse
Or fierce a need, must fare by night like that,
Five miles in darkness on a country track,
But when you do, that's what you think.

Five bells.

In Melbourne, your appetite had gone,
Your angers too; they had been leeched away
By the soft archery of summer rains
And the sponge-paws of wetness, the slow damp
That stuck the leaves of living, snailed the mind,
And showed your bones, that had been sharp with rage,
The sodden ecstasies of rectitude.
I thought of what you'd written in faint ink,
Your journal with the sawn-off lock, that stayed behind
With other things you left, all without use,
All without meaning now, except a sign
That someone had been living who now was dead:
'At Labassa. Room 6 x 8
On top of the tower; because of this, very dark
And cold in winter. Everything has been stowed
Into this room – 500 books all shapes
And colours, dealt across the floor
And over sills and on the laps of chairs;
Guns, photoes of many differant things
And differant curioes that I obtained . . .'

In Sydney, by the spent aquarium-flare
Of penny gaslight on pink wallpaper,
We argued about blowing up the world,

But you were living backward, so each night
You crept a moment closer to the breast,
And they were living, all of them, those frames
And shapes of flesh that had perplexed your youth,
And most your father, the old man gone blind,
With fingers always round a fiddle's neck,
That graveyard mason whose fair monuments
And tablets cut with dreams of piety
Rest on the bosoms of a thousand men
Staked bone by bone, in quiet astonishment
At cargoes they had never thought to bear,
These funeral-cakes of sweet and sculptured stone.

Where have you gone? The tide is over you,
The turn of midnight water's over you,
As Time is over you, and mystery,
And memory, the flood that does not flow.
You have no suburb, like those easier dead
In private berths of dissolution laid –
The tide goes over, the waves ride over you
And let their shadows down like shining hair,
But they are Water; and the sea-pinks bend
Like lilies in your teeth, but they are Weed;
And you are only part of an Idea.
I felt the wet push its black thumb-balls in,
The night you died, I felt your eardrums crack,
And the short agony, the longer dream,
The Nothing that was neither long nor short;
But I was bound, and could not go that way,
But I was blind, and could not feel your hand.
If I could find an answer, could only find
Your meaning, or could say why you were here
Who now are gone, what purpose gave you breath
Or seized it back, might I not hear your voice?

I looked out of my window in the dark
At waves with diamond quills and combs of light
That arched their mackerel-backs and smacked the sand
In the moon's drench, that straight enormous glaze,

And ships far off asleep, and Harbour-buoys
Tossing their fireballs wearily each to each,
And tried to hear your voice, but all I heard
Was a boat's whistle, and the scraping squeal
Of seabirds' voices far away, and bells,
Five bells. Five bells coldly ringing out.

Five bells.

An Inscription for Dog River*

Our general was the greatest and bravest of generals.
For his deeds, look around you on this coast –
Here is his name cut next to Ashur-Bani-Pal's,
Nebuchadnezzar's and the Roman host;
And we, though our identities have been lost,
Lacking the validity of stone or metal,
We, too, are part of his memorial,
Having been put in for the cost,

Having bestowed on him all we had to give
In battles few can recollect,
Our strength, obedience and endurance,
Our wits, our bodies, our existence,
Even our descendants' right to live –
Having given him everything, in fact,
Except respect.

*'At this point the hills approach the sea and rise high above the river; together they form a very serious obstacle which had to be negotiated by every army marching along the shore. Here the Egyptian Pharaohs therefore commemorated their successes, and their example was followed by all subsequent conquerors, Assyrian, Babylonian, Roman (and French) down to 1920' (*Steimatzky's Guide to Syria and the Lebanon*). In 1942, General Sir Thomas Blamey had an inscription cut to celebrate the capture of Damour by Australian troops under his command.

[15]

Beach Burial

Softly and humbly to the Gulf of Arabs
The convoys of dead sailors come;
At night they sway and wander in the waters far under,
But morning rolls them in the foam.

Between the sob and clubbing of the gunfire
Someone, it seems, has time for this,
To pluck them from the shallows and bury them in burrows
And tread the sand upon their nakedness;

And each cross, the driven stake of tidewood,
Bears the last signature of men,
Written with such perplexity, with such bewildered pity,
The words choke as they begin –

'*Unknown seaman*' – the ghostly pencil
Wavers and fades, the purple drips,
The breath of the wet season has washed their inscriptions
As blue as drowned men's lips,

Dead seamen, gone in search of the same landfall,
Whether as enemies they fought,
Or fought with us, or neither; the sand joins them together,
Enlisted on the other front.

El Alamein.

R. D. Fitzgerald (1902–87)

Long Since . . .

Long since I heard the muttered anger of the reef;
but it was far off even then, so far indeed
that an imagined murmur, like the ear's belief
and faith of the night, was mingled with a fuller knell
throbbing across the silence, and one could not tell
which sounds were of air stirring, which come at the mind's
    need.

And that was the old sea, alive beyond the calm
of those wide-reaching waters stifled in the lagoon –
alert, masterful waves summoning beach and palm
to be up and about and moving and ever upon quest
of new desires of the spirit, not sunk in a soft rest
only expectant of some drunkenness of the moon.

I knew it also for my own heart's call to me,
as baffling still as it would seem in the lost time
when it was loveliness on edge with melody,
elusive always and yet eternally to be sought
past any meaning of meaning or any thought of thought
now wistfully heard again in even so dulled a clime.

I turned harshly and strode back to the native town,
watched by the wooden faces, the stolid Fijian eyes,
sought my thatched doorway, entered, mechanically sat
    down,
wondering what fate was on me or what weakness took toll
that thus I must go scurrying ratwise to my hole
lest some true self should claim me with imperious cries.

The Face of the Waters

Once again the scurry of feet – those myriads
crossing the black granite; and again
laughter cruelly in pursuit; and then
the twang like a harpstring or the spring of a trap,
and the swerve on the polished surface: the soft little pads
sidling and skidding and avoiding; but soon caught up
in the hand of laughter and put back . . .

There is no release from the rack
of darkness for the unformed shape,
the unexisting thought
stretched half-and-half
in the shadow of beginning and that denser black
under the imminence of huge pylons –
the deeper nought;
but neither is there anything to escape,
or to laugh,
or to twang that string which is not a string but silence
plucked at the heart of silence.

Nor can there be a floor to the bottomless;
except in so far as conjecture must arrive,
lungs cracking, at the depth of its dive;
where downward further is further distress
with no change in it; as if a mile and an inch
are equally squeezed into a pinch,
and retreating limits of cold mind
frozen, smoothed, defined.

Out of the tension of silence (the twanged string);
from the agony of not being (that terrible laughter
tortured by darkness); out of it all
once again the tentative migration; once again
a universe on the edge of being born:
feet running fearfully out of nothing
at the core of nothing:
colour, light, life, fearfully
becoming eyes and understanding: sound becoming
    ears . . .

For eternity is not space reaching
on without end to it; not time without end to it,
nor infinity working round in a circle;
but a placeless dot enclosing nothing,
the pre-time pinpoint of impossible beginning,
enclosed by nothing, not even by emptiness –
impossible: so wholly at odds with possibilities
that, always emergent and wrestling and interlinking
they shatter it and return to it, are all of it and part of it.
It is your hand stretched out to touch your neighbour's,
and feet running through the dark, directionless like
    darkness.

Worlds that were spun adrift re-enter
that intolerable centre;
indeed the widest-looping comet
never departed from it;
it alone exists.
And though, opposing it, there persists
the enormous structure of forces, laws,
as background for other coming and going,
that's but a pattern, a phase, no pause,
of ever-being-erected, ever-growing
ideas unphysically alternative
to nothing, which is the quick. You may say hills live,
or life's the imperfect aspect of a flowing
that sorts itself as hills; much as thoughts wind
selectively through mind.

The egg-shell collapses
in the fist of the eternal instant;
all is what it was before.
Yet is that eternal instant
the pinpoint bursting into reality,
the possibilities and perhapses,
the feet scurrying on the floor.
It is the suspense also
with which the outward thrust
holds the inward surrender –
the stresses in the shell before it buckles under:
the struggle to magpie-morning and all life's clamour and
    lust;
the part breaking through the whole;
light and the clear day and so simple a goal.

from *Eleven Compositions: Roadside*

III

Having said that all the gums have not been cut
and dry sticks break beneath them; and having said
the grass is good this year, but shows a rut
developing here and there and looking red

along worn sides of hills; that as I walked
kicking up dust and powdered dung of sheep,
a hare came loping towards me, saw me, baulked,
crouched – then lost his nerve and fled with a leap;

that magpies gossiped above me on big boughs;
that tanks are three parts full though hard earth bakes;
that there are sheep, of course, a few dry cows,
not many rabbits, and I stirred no snakes;

having said this much I know and regret my loss,
whose eye falls short of my love for just this land,
too turned within for the small flower in the moss
and birds my father all but brought to his hand.

IV

Below the paved road
a suffocated soil
carries the load
with stress and with recoil

and never breathes air
nor drinks rain,
its task to hold, bear,
pressure and strain,

not nourishing seed
nor letting the roots run –
used for a strange need
foreign to the lover of sun.

There under weight and thrust
of concrete and steel
is what was live dust
that rose round boot and wheel.

Moulded and compressed
by noise, posters and print,
mind too had best
acquire the nature of flint.

Not yet the dust in man
comes to that pass;
earth, flesh for a span,
springs with the grass.

X

Wash your hands clean of guilt, and scour
your heart of the last dregs of hate.
Somewhere it is the eleventh hour,
somewhere in the world too late, too late.

There the tide ebbs towards the neap,
slacks – all its purpose at an end.
Here too the darkness turns in sleep;
stars cross their ceiling and descend.

XI

Thick dust on Paddy's lucerne, burr
and bracken and long grass,
blown from the wheels of that great stir
that men make as they pass,
paints red the roadside; but beyond
how clean are leaf and frond!

There's a new dust which you could raise
which might not stop like that
but set the last green leaf ablaze
with none to rage thereat.
Best keep your road, who travel hence,
one chain from fence to fence.

The Wind at Your Door

to Mary Gilmore

My ancestor was called on to go out –
a medical man, and one such must by law
wait in attendance on the pampered knout
and lend his countenance to what he saw,
lest the pet, patting with too bared a claw,
be judged a clumsy pussy. Bitter and hard,
see, as I see him, in that jailhouse yard.

Or see my thought of him: though time may keep
elsewhere tradition or a portrait still,
I would not feel under his cloak of sleep
if beard there or smooth chin, just to fulfil
some canon of precision. Good or ill
his blood's my own; and scratching in his grave
could find me more than I might wish to have.

Let him then be much of the middle style
of height and colouring; let his hair be dark
and his eyes green; and for that slit, the smile
that seemed inhuman, have it cruel and stark,
but grant it could be too the ironic mark
of all caught in the system – who the most,
the doctor or the flesh twined round that post?

There was a high wind blowing on that day;
for one who would not watch, but looked aside,
said that when twice he turned it blew his way
splashes of blood and strips of human hide
shaken out from the lashes that were plied
by one right-handed, one left-handed tough,
sweating at this paid task, and skilled enough.

That wind blows to your door down all these years.
Have you not known it when some breath you drew
tasted of blood? Your comfort is in arrears
of just thanks to a savagery tamed in you
only as subtler fears may serve in lieu
of thong and noose – old savagery which has built
your world and laws out of the lives it spilt.

For what was jailyard widens and takes in
my country. Fifty paces of stamped earth
stretch; and grey walls retreat and grow so thin
that towns show through and clearings – new raw birth
which burst from handcuffs – and free hands go forth
to win tomorrow's harvest from a vast
ploughland – the fifty paces of that past.

But see it through a window barred across,
from cells this side, facing the outer gate
which shuts on freedom, opens on its loss
in a flat wall. Look left now through the grate
at buildings like more walls, roofed with grey slate
or hollowed in the thickness of laid stone
each side the court where the crowd stands this noon.

One there with the officials, thick of build,
not stout, say burly (so this obstinate man
ghosts in the eyes) is he whom enemies killed
(as I was taught) because the monopolist clan
found him a grit in their smooth-turning plan,
too loyally active on behalf of Bligh.
So he got lost; and history passed him by.

But now he buttons his long coat against
the biting gusts, or as a gesture of mind,
habitual; as if to keep him fenced
from stabs of slander sticking him from behind,
sped by the schemers never far to find
in faction, where approval from one source
damns in another clubroom as of course.

This man had Hunter's confidence, King's praise;
and settlers on the starving Hawkesbury banks
recalled through twilight drifting across their days
the doctor's fee of little more than thanks
so often; and how sent by their squeezed ranks
he put their case in London. I find I lack
the hateful paint to daub him wholly black.

Perhaps my life replies to his too much
through veiling generations dropped between.
My weakness here, resentments there, may touch
old motives and explain them, till I lean
to the forgiveness I must hope may clean
my own shortcomings; since no man can live
in his own sight if it will not forgive.

Certainly I must own him whether or not
it be my will. I was made understand
this much when once, marking a freehold lot,
my papers suddenly told me it was land
granted to Martin Mason. I felt his hand
heavily on my shoulder, and knew what coil
binds life to life through bodies, and soul to soil.

There, over to one corner, a bony group
of prisoners waits; and each shall be in turn
tied by his own arms in a human loop
about the post, with his back bared to learn
the price of seeking freedom. So they earn
three hundred rippling stripes apiece, as set
by the law's mathematics against the debt.

These are the Irish batch of Castle Hill,
rebels and mutineers, my countrymen
twice over: first, because of those to till
my birthplace first, hack roads, raise roofs; and then
because their older land time and again
enrolls me through my forbears; and I claim
as origin that threshold whence we came.

One sufferer had my surname, and thereto
'Maurice', which added up to history once;
an ignorant dolt, no doubt, for all that crew
was tenantry. The breed of clod and dunce
makes patriots and true men: could I announce
that Maurice as my kin I say aloud
I'd take his irons as heraldry, and be proud.

Maurice is at the post. Its music lulls,
one hundred lashes done. If backbone shows
then play the tune on buttocks! But feel his pulse;
that's what a doctor's for; and if it goes
lamely, then dose it with these purging blows –
which have not made him moan; though, writhing there,
'Let my neck be,' he says, 'and flog me fair.'

One hundred lashes more, then rest the flail.
What says the doctor now? 'This dog won't yelp;
he'll tire you out before you'll see him fail;
here's strength to spare; go on!' Ay, pound to pulp;
yet when you've done he'll walk without your help,
and knock down guards who'd carry him being bid,
and sing no song of where the pikes are hid.

It would be well if I could find, removed
through generations back – who knows how far? –
more than a surname's thickness as a proved
bridge with that man's foundations. I need some star
of courage from his firmament, a bar
against surrenders: faith. All trials are less
than rain-blacked wind tells of that old distress.

Yet I can live with Mason. What is told
and what my heart knows of his heart, can sort
much truth from falsehood, much there that I hold
good clearly or good clouded by report;
and for things bad, ill grows where ills resort:
they were bad times. None know what in his place
they might have done. I've my own faults to face.

A. D. Hope (1907–   )

Easter Hymn

Make no mistake; there will be no forgiveness;
No voice can harm you and no hand will save;
Fenced by the magic of deliberate darkness
You walk on the sharp edges of the wave;

Trouble with soul again the putrefaction
Where Lazarus three days rotten lies content.
Your human tears will be the seed of faction,
Murder the sequel to your sacrament.

The City of God is built like other cities:
Judas negotiates the loans you float;
You will meet Caiaphas upon committees;
You will be glad of Pilate's casting vote.

Your truest lovers still the foolish virgins,
Your heart will sicken at the marriage feasts
Knowing they watch you from the darkened gardens
Being polite to your official guests.

The Gateway

Now the heart sings with all its thousand voices
To hear this city of cells, my body, sing.
The tree through the stiff clay at long last forces
Its thin strong roots and taps the secret spring.

And the sweet waters without intermission
Climb to the tips of its green tenement;
The breasts have borne the grace of their possession,
The lips have felt the pressure of content.

Here I come home: in this expected country
They know my name and speak it with delight.
I am the dream and you my gates of entry,
The means by which I waken into light.

Ascent into Hell

Little Henry, too, had a great notion of singing.
— *History of the Fairchild Family*

I, too, at the mid-point, in a well-lit wood
Of second-rate purpose and mediocre success,
Explore in dreams the never-never of childhood,
Groping in daylight for the key of darkness;

Revisit, among the morning archipelagoes,
Tasmania, my receding childish island;
Unchanged my prehistoric flora grows
Within me, marsupial territories extend:

There is the land-locked valley and the river,
The Western Tiers make distance an emotion,
The gum trees roar in the gale, the poplars shiver
At twilight, the church pines imitate an ocean.

There, in the clear night, still I listen, waking
To a crunch of sulky wheels on the distant road;
The marsh of stars reflects a starry croaking;
I hear in the pillow the sobbing of my blood

As the panic of unknown footsteps marching nearer,
Till the door opens, the inner world of panic
Nightmares that woke me to unawakening terror
Birthward resume their still inscrutable traffic.

Memory no more the backward, solid continent,
From island to island of despairing dream
I follow the dwindling soul in its ascent;
The bayonets and the pickelhauben gleam

Among the leaves, as, in the poplar tree,
They find him hiding. With an axe he stands
Above the German soldiers, hopelessly
Chopping the fingers from the climbing hands.

Or, in the well-known house, a secret door
Opens on empty rooms from which a stair
Leads down to a grey, dusty corridor,
Room after room, ominous, still and bare.

He cannot turn back, a lurking horror beckons
Round the next corner, beyond each further door.
Sweating with nameless anguish then he wakens;
Finds the familiar walls blank as before.

Chased by wild bulls, his legs stick fast with terror.
He reaches the fence at last – the fence falls flat.
Choking, he runs, the trees he climbs will totter.
Or the cruel horns, like telescopes, shoot out.

At his fourth year the waking life turns inward.
Here on his Easter Island the stone faces
Rear meaningless monuments of hate and dread.
Dreamlike within the dream real names and places

Survive. His mother comforts him with her body
Against the nightmare of the lions and tigers.
Again he is standing in his father's study
Lying about his lie, is whipped, and hears

His scream of outrage, valid to this day.
In bed, he fingers his stump of sex, invents
How he took off his clothes and ran away,
Slit up his belly with various instruments;

To brood on this was a deep abdominal joy
Still recognized as a feeling at the core
Of love – and the last genuine memory
Is singing 'Jesus Loves Me' – then, no more!

Beyond is a lost country and in vain
I enter that mysterious territory.
Lit by faint hints of memory lies the plain
Where from its Null took shape this conscious I

Which backward scans the dark – But at my side
The unrecognized Other Voice speaks in my ear,
The voice of my fear, the voice of my unseen guide;
'Who are we, stranger? What are we doing here?'

And through the uncertain gloom, sudden I see
Beyond remembered time the imagined entry,
The enormous Birth-gate whispering, *'per me,
per me si va tra la perduta gente.'*

The Pleasure of Princes

What pleasures have great princes? These: to know
Themselves reputed mad with pride or power;
To speak few words – few words and short bring low
This ancient house, that city with flame devour;

To make old men, their father's enemies,
Drunk on the vintage of the former age;
To have great painters show their mistresses
Naked to the succeeding time; engage

The cunning of able, treacherous ministers
To serve, despite themselves, the cause they hate,
And leave a prosperous kingdom to their heirs
Nursed by the caterpillars of the state;

To keep their spies in good men's hearts; to read
The malice of the wise, and act betimes;
To hear the Grand Remonstrances of greed,
Led by the pure; cheat justice of her crimes;

To beget worthless sons and, being old,
By starlight climb the battlements, and while
The pacing sentry hugs himself for cold,
Keep vigil like a lover, muse and smile,

And think, to see from the grim castle steep
The midnight city below rejoice and shine:
'There my great demon grumbles in his sleep
And dreams of his destruction, and of mine.'

The Death of the Bird

For every bird there is this last migration:
Once more the cooling year kindles her heart;
With a warm passage to the summer station
Love pricks the course in lights across the chart.

Year after year a speck on the map, divided
By a whole hemisphere, summons her to come;
Season after season, sure and safely guided,
Going away she is also coming home.

And being home, memory becomes a passion
With which she feeds her brood and straws her nest,
Aware of ghosts that haunt the heart's possession
And exiled love mourning within the breast.

The sands are green with a mirage of valleys;
The palm-tree casts a shadow not its own;
Down the long architrave of temple or palace
Blows a cool air from moorland scarps of stone.

And day by day the whisper of love grows stronger;
That delicate voice, more urgent with despair,
Custom and fear constraining her no longer,
Drives her at last on the waste leagues of air.

A vanishing speck in those inane dominions,
Single and frail, uncertain of her place,
Alone in the bright host of her companions,
Lost in the blue unfriendliness of space,

She feels it close now, the appointed season:
The invisible thread is broken as she flies;
Suddenly, without warning, without reason,
The guiding spark of instinct winks and dies.

Try as she will, the trackless world delivers
No way, the wilderness of light no sign,
The immense and complex map of hills and rivers
Mocks her small wisdom with its vast design.

And darkness rises from the eastern valleys,
And the winds buffet her with their hungry breath,
And the great earth, with neither grief nor malice,
Receives the tiny burden of her death.

The Coasts of Cerigo

Half of the land, conscious of love and grief,
Half of the sea, cold creatures of the foam,
Mermaids still haunt and sing among the coves.
Sailors, who catch them basking on the reef,
Say they make love like women, and that some
Will die if once deserted by their loves.

Off shore, in deeper water, where the swell
Smokes round their crests, the cliffs of coral plunge
Fathom by fathom to the ocean floor.
There, rooted to the ooze-bed, as they tell,
Strange sister to the polyp and the sponge,
To holothurian and madrepore,

The Labra wallows in her bath of time
And, drowned in timeless sleep, displays the full
Grace of a goddess risen from the wave.
Small scarlet-crabs with awkward gestures climb
Through the black seaweed drifting from her skull.
Her ladylegs gape darkly as a cave,

And through the coral clefts a gleam and gloom
Reveal the fronded arch, the pelvic gate;
Spotted and barred, the amorous fish swim in.
But in that hollow, mocking catacomb
Their love-songs echo and reverberate
A senseless clamour and a wordless din.

The love-trap closes on its gullible prey
Despite their sobs, despite their ecstasies.
Brilliant with tropic bands and stripes, they dart
Through a delicious juice which eats away
Their scales and soon dissolves their goggle eyes
And melts the milt-sac and the pulsing heart.

The divers on these coasts have cruel hands;
Their lives are hard; they do not make old bones;
The brutal masters send them down too deep.
But sometimes, as he combs the clefts and sands,
Among the oyster-beds and bearded stones
One comes upon the Labra fast asleep

And throws away his knife, his bag of pearl,
To take her in his arms and wrench her free.
Their bodies cling together as they rise
Spinning and drifting in the ocean swirl.
The seamen haul them in and stand to see
The exquisite, fabled creature as she dies.

But while in air they watch her choke and drown,
Enchanted by her beauty, they forget
The body of their comrade at her side,
From whose crushed lungs the bright blood oozing down
Jewel by ruby jewel from the wet
Deck drops and merges in the turquoise tide.

Advice to Young Ladies

AUC 334: about this date
For a sexual misdemeanour, which she denied,
The vestal virgin Postumia was tried.
Livy records it among affairs of state.

They let her off: it seems she was perfectly pure;
The charge arose because some thought her talk
Too witty for a young girl, her eyes, her walk
Too lively, her clothes too smart to be demure.

The Pontifex Maximus, summing up the case,
Warned her in future to abstain from jokes,
To wear less modish and more pious frocks.
She left the court reprieved, but in disgrace.

What then? With her the annalist is less
Concerned than what the men achieved that year:
Plots, quarrels, crimes, with oratory to spare!
I see Postumia with her dowdy dress,

Stiff mouth and listless step; I see her strive
To give dull answers. She had to knuckle down.
A vestal virgin who scandalized that town
Had fair trial, then they buried her alive.

Alive, bricked up in suffocating dark,
A ration of bread, a pitcher if she was dry,
Preserved the body they did not wish to die
Until her mind was quenched to the last spark.

How many the black maw has swallowed in its time!
Spirited girls who would not know their place;
Talented girls who found that the disgrace
Of being a woman made genius a crime;

How many others, who would not kiss the rod
Domestic bullying broke or public shame?
Pagan or Christian, it was much the same:
Husbands, St Paul declared, rank next to God.

Livy and Paul, it may be, never knew
That Rome was doomed; each spoke of her with pride.
Tacitus, writing after both had died,
Showed that whole fabric rotten through and through.

Historians spend their lives and lavish ink
Explaining how great commonwealths collapse
From great defects of policy – perhaps
The cause is sometimes simpler than they think.

It may not seem so grave an act to break
Postumia's spirit as Galileo's, to gag
Hypatia as crush Socrates, or drag
Joan as Giordano Bruno to the stake.

Can we be sure? Have more states perished, then,
For having shackled the enquiring mind,
Than those who, in their folly not less blind,
Trusted the servile womb to breed free men?

Lament for the Murderers

Where are they now, the genteel murderers
And gentlemanly sleuths, whose household names
Made crime a club for well-bred amateurs;
Slaughter the cosiest of indoor games?

Where are the long week-ends, the sleepless nights
We spent treading the dance in dead men's shoes,
And all the ratiocinative delights
Of matching motives and unravelling clues,

The public-spirited corpse in evening dress,
Blood like an order across the snowy shirt,
Killings contrived with no unseemly mess
And only rank outsiders getting hurt:

A fraudulent banker or a blackmailer,
The rich aunt dragging out her spiteful life,
The lovely bitch, the cheap philanderer
Bent on seducing someone else's knife?

Where are those headier methods of escape
From the dull fare of peace: the well-spiced dish
Of torture, violence and brutal rape,
Perversion, madness and still queerer fish?

All gone! That dear delicious make-believe,
The armchair blood sports and dare-devil dreams.
We dare not even sleep now, dare not leave
The armchair. What we hear are real screams.

Real people, whom we know, have really died.
No one knows why. The nightmares have come true.
We ring the police: A voice says 'Homicide!
Just wait your turn. When we get round to you

You will be sorry you were born. Don't call
For help again: a murderer saves his breath.
When guilt consists in being alive at all
Justice becomes the other name for Death.'

Loving Kind

Loving Kind went by the way,
Hapless Loving Kind,
Up and down, by night and day,
Her true love to find.

Roving eye and nimble tongue
All her paths pursue:
How should she, and she so young,
Know false love from true?

Some by grace she would compel;
None would she deny:
How shall I my true love tell
Only passing by?

Sober heart and prudent mind
Scorn her and reprove:
How should she by loving find
Any truth in love?

Yet she smiled and smiling said:
Though my love I see
Except I take him to my bed,
How shall he know me?

Inscription for a War

Stranger, go tell the Spartans
we died here obedient to their commands.
   – Inscription at Thermopylae

Linger not, stranger; shed no tear;
Go back to those who sent us here.

We are the young they drafted out
To wars their folly brought about.

Go tell those old men, safe in bed,
We took their orders and are dead.

Elizabeth Riddell (1909–   )

The Letter

I take my pen in hand
        there was a meadow
beside a field of oats, beside a wood,
beside a road, beside a day spread out
green at the edges, yellow at the heart.
The dust lifted a little, a finger's breadth;
the word of the wood pigeon travelled slow,
a slow half-pace behind the tick of time.

To tell you I am well and thinking of you
and of the walk through the meadow, and of another walk
along the neat piled ruin of the town
under a pale heaven empty of all but death
and rain beginning. The river ran beside.

It has been a long time since I wrote. I have no news.
I put my head between my hands and hope
my heart will choke me. I put out my hand
to touch you and touch air. I turn to sleep
and find a nightmare, hollowness and fear.

And by the way, I have had no letter now
For eight weeks, it must be
a long eight weeks
because you have nothing to say, nothing at all,
not even to record your emptiness
or guess what's to become of you, without love.

I know that you have cares
ashes to shovel, broken glass to mend
and many a cloth to patch before the sunset.

Write to me soon and tell me how you are
if you still tremble, sweat and glower, still stretch
a hand for me at dusk, play me the tune,
show me the leaves and towers, the lamb, the rose.

Because I always wish to hear of you
and feel my heart swell and the blood run out
at the ungraceful syllable of your name
said through the scent of stocks, the little snore of fire,
the shoreless waves of symphony, the murmuring night.

I will end this letter now. I am yours with love.
Always with love, with love.

Forebears

I *The Map*

O search the heart and belly you may find
The map of blood and it may have some meaning
But as for me as spring burns into summer and the blind
Suns follow each other to indifferent dark
I will embrace my other cousin, death,
Who long ago lay with my ancestors.

II *The Reverend Edward Smith*

By Waggon Hill he went
Forgiving his parish,
His left and right neighbours,
His wife in her narrow bed
The sheets to her chin,
The keeper of the inn,
The cold man in the watch-house
His cook and acquaintance,
Squire Rat in his high boots
And Lord and Lady Mouse.

But they not so lavish
With tender excuses
Refused to condone
His meagre black legs,
His long cold fingers,
The sighing of his prayers
On light bright mornings,
His hauntings and warnings.
And now he is dead
They avoid the stone
And the thin rim of grass
On his pious bone.

III *John Teague*

He twined the country like a briar in the fair weather
But when the autumn gales
Tore at the stubborn roots of rocks and trees
Who lit his lamp?
For other men left home to live like saints or die like dogs
But he to practise divination.

The old women would pay him a penny to twitch
The bowels with fear
(Somewhat better than a witch
Because at least a man)
But the farmer would not hear
Ill omen of the harvest till it failed
And then they set the louts, the priests and fire,
The girls crying, and horses and men, the bishop in red
With hounds and prayer to run and read him out.

The village shuddered back into its dust
And he with blood about his head
Threaded the country like a briar,
But when the gales of autumn shook the world
Who lit his lamp?

He could endure the rods across his back
But not the woman and child beside the hearth.
He was John Teague
Who left his cobbler's shop
To practise divination.

   IV *Montfort Lee and Peter Cockerill*

When the ships *Nimbus* and *Pacific Fortune*
Slid under the southing star
To Hobart Town came I in the blood of Montfort Lee
And Peter Cockerill
(Of Bankbourne in this parish, deeply mourned)
Came I in their round pale eyes and pale smooth hair
And with them planted quinces, pears and wheat,
And with them rose at dawn to be a farmer,
And with them drank
(Gentry's white cuffs below the jacket sleeves)
Cider at Norfolk.
I was the seed they sowed when nothing stirred
Across the river but a kingfisher
Abreast of morning.
(Who laid the hopfields wide and planted vines,
And built a house of stone, and sailed a boat,
And went to marriages and funerals,
And matched each other's daughters with their sons,
And rode their horses by the willow-trees,
And seldom read a book or sang a song.)

V *Mary Lomax*

Here is the woman with the face of pearl and rose,
The great madonna of misunderstanding, she
With laces at her wrist and the unearthly glow
Of ritual in her evening's arbour pose.
My mother's mother's mother, she in paint
And gilt by secondary artists set
Upon the wall. And all her axioms lie
As shattered mirrors round her, and the faint
Tinkle of teacups dies, and dies away.
Nothing is left of all she had to say.

VI *The Man from Richmond*

The man from Richmond ran before
The lads upon his stumbling heel
Past the church and past the store,
Past the smith and the millwheel,
Past the rhododendrons drowned
Pale, pale, under the rain,
Ran, ran until he found
Shelter where the hawthorned lane
Turned to the meadow. There he lay,
Put his cheek to the earth and wept,
And cries of idiot died away,
And the man slept.
He the father, he the fool,
Caught between the hill and stream,
Between the cliff and the shallow pool,
The people and the dream.
He the zany, he the clod
Lying under the hawthorn-tree
Wept because he was not God.
He was I and I am he.

William Hart-Smith (1911–   )

Fishing

Heads moved in a wide, slow semi-circle
Among the many levels of waves.

I watched men growing out of the water,
Naked brown men from water warmer than the wind,
Moving backwards, striving to the beach;

And I waded out and groped deep for a hold
On the drowned rope and set my back and set my arms
To work with them, and saw

The bag come riding from the surf, the swollen
Bag spitting thin silver.

Bathymeter

Those who have descended to the nethermost deeps
of the ocean sealed in a bell
past where the last blue-violet creeps

imperceptibly away, and have hung
suspended on a filament in utter dark,
while above them rung on rung

the colours of the spectrum ladder rise,
say that the fish have lights
like rows of portholes, dots around their eyes,

headlamps of fluorescent studs,
or lanterns hung on poles,
and the darkness is alive with moving buds

of phosphorescence; fish with dim-lit sails,
shrimps that explode
in an enemy's face, and clouds of luminous snails.

And those who have been up in a balloon
so high the pale blue sky goes dark,
and darker, and the sun and moon

burn pitilessly, say
the myriad stars appear
shining at high noon of the brightest day.

In a liquid atmosphere that presses tight
with a multitude of tons,
fish scrawl an aimless script direct in light;

while high above, a multitude of suns
in eternal night
dance to a cosmic tune. And midway runs,

precariously swung between extremes,
our film of atmosphere, where light's diffused,
a narrow equipoise of pressure, heat and cold. It seems

this dance of stars in solemn time
and fish in swing is certain proof the Lord,
whoever he be, cannot resist a rhyme.

Birth

I cannot resist now and then being born
into the dark world of Theatre.

I like to settle down in my seat
and watch event succeed event

on a two-dimensional sheet,
I like to let myself identify

with all the happenings that sequence by
and then get up and die into the Street.

Ambrosia

He lifted a drop of ambrosia
on a length of brittle straw

and let the bead of nectar run
back along the straw

towards His hand.
Lifted the straw

and tilted it towards the earth again until where the
droplet gathered

seven colours flashed.
With it he touched

a creature's being,
the creature of all creatures

that he most loved and treasured.
One assumes

the quantity was not precisely measured.

Observation

Now and then concentrating
on the very small,

focusing my attention
on a very small area

like this crack in sandstone
perpetually wet with seepage,

getting so close
to moss, liverwort, and fern

it becomes a forest
with wild beasts in it,

birds in the branches
and crickets piping,

cicadas shrilling.
Someone seeing me

staring so fixedly
at nothing

might be excused
for thinking me vague, abstracted,

lost in introspection.
No! I am awake, absorbed,

just looking in a different direction.

Altamira

One held the resined pinebranch
which gave a pulsing yellow flame
with a taper of black smoke,
while the other painted
using a stick, the end of it chewed
so that the fibres held the pigment
ground of ochreous clays and haematite
mixed to a paste with fat and human spittle.

In the deep recesses of those caves
as in the imagination itself
bringing the outside world inside
under control,
captured the bison and the deer.

To make the thin straight line of a spear-shaft
in the throat of a deer,
a fragment of charcoal on the palette.
Used the straight-edge of a bone
to steady his hand.

Douglas Stewart (1913–85)

from *Glencoe*

15.

Sigh, wind in the pine;
River, weep as you flow;
Terrible things were done
Long, long ago.

In daylight golden and mild
After the night of Glencoe
They found the hand of a child
Lying upon the snow.

Lopped by the sword to the ground
Or torn by wolf or fox,
That was the snowdrop they found
Among the granite rocks.

Oh, life is fierce and wild
And the heart of the earth is stone,
And the hand of a murdered child
Will not bear thinking on.

Sigh, wind in the pine,
Cover it over with snow;
But terrible things were done
Long, long ago.

The Night of the Moths

The giant moths like sparrows! So many drowned
On the stony mountain struggling out of the ground,
So many battered from the air by the wind and the storm
Where the black rain beats on Bindo; yet still they swarm
From the tunnel in the clay, from the dark wet
    undergrowth,
Through the night and the trees, great whirring moth by
    moth.

The midnight hides their long clear rainy wings,
Their bodies of gold; blindly the black earth flings
Its passion of blind black life to meet the rain;
And one with the storm, with the trees as they shudder and
    strain,
One with the mountain shambling in night and stone,
Up the dark ridge they fly, and they are gone.

The Silkworms

All their lives in a box! What generations,
What centuries of masters, not meaning to be cruel
But needing their labour, taught these creatures such
    patience
That now though sunlight strikes on the eye's dark jewel
Or moonlight breathes on the wing they do not stir
But like the ghosts of moths crouch silent there.

Look it's a child's toy! There is no lid even,
They can climb, they can fly, and the whole world's their
    tree;
But hush, they say in themselves, we are in prison.
There is no word to tell them that they are free,
And they are not; ancestral voices bind them
In dream too deep for wind or word to find them.

Even in the young, each like a little dragon
Ramping and green upon his mulberry leaf,
So full of life, it seems, the voice has spoken:
They hide where there is food, where they are safe,
And the voice whispers, 'Spin the cocoon,
Sleep, sleep, you shall be wrapped in me soon.'

Now is their hour, when they wake from that long swoon;
Their pale curved wings are marked in a pattern of leaves,
Shadowy for trees, white for the dance of the moon;
And when on summer nights the buddleia gives
Its nectar like lilac wine for insects mating
They drink its fragrance and shiver, impatient with waiting,

They stir, they think they will go. Then they remember
It was forbidden, forbidden, ever to go out;
The Hands are on guard outside like claps of thunder,
The ancestral voice says Don't, and they do not.
Still the night calls them to unimaginable bliss
But there is terror around them, the vast, the abyss,

And here is the tribe that they know, in their known place,
They are gentle and kind together, they are safe for ever,
And all shall be answered at last when they embrace.
White moth moves closer to moth, lover to lover.
There is that pang of joy on the edge of dying –
Their soft wings whirr, they dream that they are flying.

B Flat

Sing softly, Muse, the Reverend Henry White
Who floats through time as lightly as a feather
Yet left one solitary gleam of light
Because he was the Selborne naturalist's brother

And told him once how on warm summer eves
When moonlight filled all Fyfield to the brim
And yearning owls were hooting to their loves
On church and barn and oak-tree's leafy limb

He took a common half-a-crown pitch-pipe
Such as the masters used for harpsichords
And through the village trod with silent step
Measuring the notes of those melodious birds

And found that each one sang, or rather hooted,
Precisely in the measure of B flat.
And that is all that history has noted;
We know no more of Henry White than that.

So, softly, Muse, in harmony and conformity
Pipe up for him and all such gentle souls
Thus in the world's enormousness, enormity,
So interested in music and in owls;

For though we cannot claim his crumb of knowledge
Was worth much more than virtually nil
Nor hail him for vast enterprise or courage,
Yet in my mind I see him walking still

With eager ear beneath his clerical hat
Through Fyfield village sleeping dark and blind,
Oh surely as he piped his soft B flat
The most harmless, the most innocent of mankind.

John Blight (1913–   )

Cormorants

The sea has it this way: if you see
cormorants, they are the pattern for the eye.
In the sky, on the rocks, in the water – shags!
To think of them every way: I see them, oily rags
flung starboard from some tramp and washed
onto rocks, flung up by the waves, squashed
into sock-shapes with the foot up; sooty birds
wearing white, but not foam-white; swearing, not words,
but blaspheming with swastika-gesture, wing-hinge to nose;
ugly grotesqueries, all in a shag's pose.
And beautifully ugly for their being shags,
not partly swans. When the eye searches for rags,
it does not seek muslin, white satin; nor,
for its purpose, does the sea adorn shags more.

Mangrove

I saw its periscope in the tide;
its torpedo-seed seeking the soft side
of the island, the grey mud-bank.
And, where it touched, it seemed the land sank
with its trees exploding from water; the green
mangroves' fountainhead of leaves bursting, seen
like a mushroom-top of detritus and spray.
Today, in my boat, at the close end of the bay,
I saw its dark devastations; islet and spit
sunk in the flat high tide. Where these war-seeds hit,
gaps of horizon and sea; then trees . . . gaps . . . trees
. . . like men on a flushed foredeck. No ease:
the drab olive-green swarming everywhere;
troops of the mangroves, uniform, everywhere.

Conflagration

The man raced wildly through a burning
doorway. Unlike a shadow which I
saw entering yesterday – a
shadow coolly sheltering life.

There were staccato
cracking members where yesterday
I passed by listening to a flute's
leisure.

The man whom I saw
push through the front door of the flames
was red-faced, his hair black as the
coals. The youth I glimpsed yesterday
was fair-skinned as sunlight which spills
through an unlatched entrance on a
day of sunshine.

I don't think the
two men whom I saw glimpsed the same
face of the woman-tenant there.
Each time I passed, each time a woman
bared her face through a window. I
had never had grace and fear told
me so immeasurably in
words.

But nobody spoke. One day
there was that yellow light and peace,
the next saw red, a conflagration.

The Disarrayed

Forgetting how to observe, what
to observe, in my ageing years
. . . a rose, or a red scarf on a
young woman whom winter compels
to wear cloaking habit . . .

                              I now
recall my sisters with their dolls
and the obscenity from which
I shrank, seeing the dolls unclothed;
these looking like pullets my father
had beheaded and plucked for the
pot. Somehow the dolls always lost
their heads, or their heads seemed severed.

Later I thought of Gogol and
the theatre – but always this
unease in the presence of the
disarrayed.

              Imagine how I
feel now in my city's treeless
wastes strewn with the weeks' wraps
thrown down.

All such Victorian thinking!
but there is some nostalgia
for those years of my parents'
parents in the old photographs
– rich man and poor man alike in
suits, and so many rows of
women in great hats that must have
looked like gardens of flowers
to a boy climbing a tree by
the roadside, perched in a branch
above them.

Even close summer's
deep décolletés would not startle
but promise buds in spring – and who
even in those years of decorum
didn't pick bunches of rosebuds?

Kenneth Mackenzie (1913–55)

The Snake

Withdrawing from the amorous grasses
from the warm and luscious water
the snake is soul untouched by both
nor does the fire of day through which it passes
mark it or cling. Immaculate navigator
it carries death within its mouth.

Soul is the snake that moves at will
through all the nets of circumstance
like the wind that nothing stops,
immortal movement in a world held still
by rigid anchors of intent or chance
and ropes of fear and stays of hopes.

It is the source of all dispassion
the voiceless life above communion
secret as the spring of wind
nor does it know the shames of self-confession
the weakness that enjoys love's coarse dominion
or the betrayals of the mind.

Soul is the snake the cool viator
sprung from a shadow on the grass
quick and intractable as breath
gone as it came like the everlasting water
reflecting god in immeasurable space –
and in its mouth it carries death.

Caesura

Sometimes at night when the heart stumbles and stops
a full second endless the endless steps
that lead me on through this time terrain
without edges and beautiful terrible
are gone never to proceed again.

Here is a moment of enormous trouble
when the kaleidoscope sets unalterable
and at once without meaning without motion
like a stalled aeroplane in the middle sky
ready to fall down into a waiting ocean.

Blackness rises. Am I now to die
and feel the steps no more and not see day
break out its answering smile of hail all's well
from east full round to east and hear the bird
whistle all creatures that on earth do dwell?

Not now. Old heart has stopped to think of a word
as someone in a dream by far too weird
to be unlikely feels a kiss and stops
to praise all heaven stumbling in all his senses . . .
and suddenly hears again the endless steps.

Two Trinities

Are you ready? soul said again
smiling deep in the dark
where mind and I live passionately
grain rasping across grain
in a strangled question-mark
– or so we have lived lately.

I looked through the hollow keyhole
at my wife not young any more
with my signature on her forehead
and her spirit hers and whole
unsigned by me – as before
we knew each other, and wed.

I looked at my grown daughter
cool and contained as a flower
whose bees I shall not be among –
vivid as white spring water
full of womanish power
like the first phrases of a song.

I looked at my son, and wept
in my mouth's cave to see
the seed ready for sowing
and the harvest unready to be reaped –
green fruit shocked from the tree,
the bird killed on the wing.

Well? soul said and I said,
Mind and I are at one
to go with you now – finally
joined now to be led –
for our place here is gone:
we are not among those three.

Soul said, *Now come with me.*

An Old Inmate

Joe Green Joe Green O how are you doing today?
I'm well, he said, and the bones of his head looked noble.
That night they wheeled Joe Green on a whisper away
but his voice rang on in the ward: I'm a terrible trouble
to all you girls. I make you work for your pay.
If I 'ad my way I'd see that they paid you double.

Joe Green Joe Green for eighty-two years and more
you walked the earth of your grandad's farm down-river
where oranges bigger than suns grow back from the shore
in the dark straight groves. Your love for life was a fever
that polished your eye and glowed in your cheek the more
the more you aged and pulsed in your voice for ever.

Joe Green looked down on his worked-out hands with scorn
and tears of age and sickness and pride and wonder
lay on his yellow cheek where the grooves were worn
shallow and straight: but the scorn of his look was tender
like a lover's who hears reproaches meet to be borne
and his voice no more than echoed its outdoor thunder:

Gi' me the good old days and the old-time folk.
You don't find that sort now you clever young fellers.
Wireless motorbikes all this American talk
and the pitchers and atom-bombs. O' course it follers
soon you'll forget 'ow to read or think or walk –
and there won't be one o' you sleeps at night on your
    pillers!

Joe Green Joe Green let us hear what your grandad said
when you were a lad and the oranges not yet planted
on the deep soil where the dark wild children played
the land that Governor King himself had granted
fifteen decades ago that the Green men made
a mile-square Eden where nothing that lived there wanted.

Joe Green lay back and smiled at the western sun:
'Fear God and the women, boy,' was his only lesson,
'and love 'em – but on the 'ole just leave 'em alone,
the women specially.' Maybe I didn't listen
all of the time. A man ain't made of stone . . .
But I done my share of praying and fearing and kissing.

No. I 'ad no dad nor mum of me own –
not to remember – but still I'd a good upbringing.
The gran'ma raised thirty-two of us all alone
child and grandchild . . . Somewhere a bell goes ringing.
Steps and the shielded lanterns come and are gone.
The old voice rocks with laughter and tears and singing.

Gi' me the good old days . . . Joe Green Joe Green
how are you doing tonight? Is it cold work dying?
Not 'alf so cold as some of the frosts I've seen
out Sackville way . . . The voice holds fast defying
sleep and silence, the whisper and the trifold screen
and the futile difficult sounds of his old girl's crying.

John Manifold (1915–85)

For Comrade Katharine

I

That moment on my mind
Etched you, with one arm raised
Tautening the breasts I praised,
Dark on the street-lit blind;

Moment and pose combined
Luxuriously appraised
Revealed to me amazed
Love's rare and perfect kind;

Not just the ornament
Of leisure and content
But sinewy and keen

To walk in the cold and share
The tang as if marine
Of hatred in the air.

II

Give me what of death you hold
In your loins and lips and hands;
Act and word are contraband
At a frontier so controlled.

So in earth and darkness rolled
Sleeps the harvest of wild lands
And again in summer stands
Vigorously manifold.

Hands from writing, lips from speech
Turn to festival with yours,
Mingle, play, and sleep, and then

Like the sailor to the beach
Fresh with our united force
Rally to our task again.

The Last Scab of Hawarth

Why does the fire burn high to me
   When your end burns so low?
Maybe it's of the coal I cut
   Fifteen years ago.

What are the sparks that fly so far
   And flash against the dark?
They might be eyes that would not see
   When we went out to work.

There's five men went scabbing then
   And thought their work was well,
And one died mad and two died sane
   And one that's dead in jail.

There's five men went scabbing then
   And thought their work was fit,
And sane or mad there's four men dead
   And one that's living yet.

And maybe if they haddna worked
   When all the rest stood by,
The coal that's aye so cheap to work
   Might not be so dear to buy.

And maybe if they haddna worked
   When all the rest stood back,
The fire might keep and the kids might sleep
   And the night be not so black.

[63]

There's two died sane and two died mad
   And the one that's last is me.
And he went with a clothesline in his hand
   To look for a leaning tree.

Fife Tune

for Sixth Platoon, 308th ITC

One morning in spring
We marched from Devizes
All shapes and all sizes
Like beads on a string,
But yet with a swing
We trod the bluemetal
And full of high fettle
We started to sing.

She ran down the stair
A twelve-year-old darling
And laughing and calling
She tossed her bright hair;
Then silent to stare
At the men flowing past her –
There were all she could master
Adoring her there.

It's seldom I'll see
A sweeter or prettier;
I doubt we'll forget her
In two years or three,
And lucky he'll be
She takes for a lover
While we are far over
The treacherous sea.

Fencing School

White to the neck he glides and plunges
But black above, no human foe
Pity for whom could rob my lunges
Of their direction. Faceless, so,

He is no fellow but a show
Of motion purposed to withstand
The blade that sets my nerves aglow
And sings exultant in the hand.

Thus each withdrawn and wide alert,
Focussed on self from hilt to heel,
Nothing breaks in to controvert

The single aim. I only feel
The sinews of my wrist assert
The tremor of engaging steel.

The Tomb of Lt John Learmonth, AIF

'At the end on Crete he took to the hills, and said he'ld fight it out with
only a revolver. He was a great soldier.'
— One of his men in a letter

This is not sorrow, this is work: I build
A cairn of words over a silent man,
My friend John Learmonth whom the Germans killed.

There was no word of hero in his plan;
Verse should have been his love and peace his trade,
But history turned him to a partisan.

Far from the battle as his bones are laid
Crete will remember him. Remember well,
Mountains of Crete, the Second Field Brigade!

Say Crete, and there is little more to tell
Of muddle tall as treachery, despair
And black defeat resounding like a bell;

But bring the magnifying focus near
And in contempt of muddle and defeat
The old heroic virtues still appear.

Australian blood where hot and icy meet
(James Hogg and Lermontov were of his kin)
Lie still and fertilise the fields of Crete.

*   *   *

Schoolboy, I watched his ballading begin:
Billy and bullocky and billabong,
Our properties of childhood, all were in.

I heard the air though not the undersong,
The fierceness and resolve; but all the same
They're the tradition, and tradition's strong.

Swagman and bushranger die hard, die game,
Die fighting, like that wild colonial boy –
Jack Dowling, says the ballad, was his name.

He also spun his pistol like a toy,
Turned to the hills like wolf or kangaroo,
And faced destruction with a bitter joy.

His freedom gave him nothing else to do
But set his back against his family tree
And fight the better for the fact he knew

He was as good as dead. Because the sea
Was closed and the air dark and the land lost,
'They'll never capture me alive,' said he.

*   *   *

That's courage chemically pure, uncrossed
With sacrifice or duty or career,
Which counts and pays in ready coin the cost

Of holding course. Armies are not its sphere
Where all's contrived to achieve its counterfeit;
It swears with discipline, its volunteer.

I could as hardly make a moral fit
Around it as around a lightning flash.
There is no moral, that's the point of it,

No moral. But I'm glad of this panache
That sparkles, as from flint, from us and steel,
True to no crown nor presidential sash

Nor flag nor fame. Let others mourn and feel
He died for nothing: nothings have their place.
While thus the kind and civilised conceal

This spring of unsuspected inward grace
And look on death as equals, I am filled
With queer affection for the human race.

David Campbell (1915–79)

Men in Green

There were fifteen men in green,
Each with a tommy-gun,
Who leapt into my plane at dawn;
We rose to meet the sun.

Our course lay to the east. We climbed
Into the break of day,
Until the jungle far beneath
Like a giant fossil lay.

We climbed towards the distant range
Where two white paws of cloud
Clutched at the shoulders of the pass.
The green men laughed aloud.

They did not fear the ape-like cloud
That climbed the mountain crest
And rode the currents of the air
And hid the pass in mist.

They did not fear the summer's sun
In whose hot centre lie
A hundred hissing cannon shells
For the unwatchful eye.

And when at Dobadura we
Set down, each turned to raise
His thumb towards the open sky
In mockery and praise.

But fifteen men in jungle green
Rose from the kunai grass
To come aboard, and my green men
In silence watched them pass:
It seemed they looked upon themselves
In a prophetic glass.

They were some leaned on a stick
And some on stretchers lay,
But few walked on their own two feet
In the early green of day.

They had not feared the ape-like cloud
That climbed the mountain crest;
They had not feared the summer's sun
With bullets for their breast.

Their eyes were bright, their looks were dull,
Their skin had turned to clay.
Nature had met them in the night
And stalked them in the day.

And I think still of men in green
On the Soputa track
With fifteen spitting tommy-guns
To keep a jungle back.

Who Points the Swallow

Love who points the swallow home
And scarves the russet at his throat,
Dreaming in the needle's eye,
Guide us through the maze of glass
Where the forceful cannot pass,
With your silent clarity.

[69]

There where blood and sap are one,
Thrush's heart and daisy's root
Keep the measure of the dance,
Though within their cage of bone
Griefs and tigers stalk alone,
Locked in private arrogance.

Lay the shadow of our fear
With the brilliance of your light,
Naked we can meet the storm,
Travellers who journeyed far
To find you at our own front door,
O love who points the swallow home.

from *Works and Days*

III Harvesting

In early ear oats glaze; wheat is hard green,
Burnishing to a furnace glow in summer.
When the stalk snaps clean, she's ready. Like a dinosaur,
The header munches a swathe and the fence is clear.

The blue days itch with silver. Blond and long,
Straw bows to diamond knives. Put a hand in the bin
And feel the good full grain come piping in.
Towards dusk by the dump, some sheila's singing a song.

The bag-sewers are busy: it could go fourteen,
The way they twitch the ears and needles fly
In loops of silver. And warmly the rich voice sings
Over the harvest field to a rose-green sky.

XI Weather

There's a time the grass turns pink, the seed is setting.
Shorn ewes rule lines on hillsides with lambs at foot.
Then it blows ten days from the west, the sheep-camps
   yellow,
And it's not the best year old hands remember yet.

– Reminds me of '57 . . . A hot dry summer
Puts heart in the stock . . . Could do with an inch or two
To fill the ears out . . . It's when it comes that counts . . .
Heads shake and the cattle market takes a tumble.

Rain from high skies. Sheep newly-shorn are shedded:
Cooper's lost two hundred. Bullfrogs bellow from dams
And dabchick nests float incubating. Water
Fills crescent hoof-marks. – A terrible year for fires!

from *Starting from Central Station*

IX Angina

He feared angina from his thirtieth year:
A doctor, he knew what to fear.
On the stair I saw him stop,
Take his pulse and climb the mountain top.

Drought, boredom, loneliness, could bring it on,
And his unlikely son:
Deeper than Eros' dart
Care struck my father's heart.

On Kismet, his roan mare,
he cut out cow and steer;
Then chained up his blue heeler, and
For fear of germs, scrubbed hand on hand.

I do the same myself now. But in Scot
He said at our last row, 'You'll nae forget,'
And climbed to fix a mill. At seventy-three
Was it angina or did he die of me?

Sugar Loaf

> I see the whole huge hill
>   in the small pool's stomach
>
> – Ted Hughes, 'Sugar Loaf'

Also it could prove serious for the pool,
Reflecting in its tilted glass
The hill, a tall giant, trustful
As a bloodhound but simple, tossing clouds about,
At one with each sunken pebble.

The pool is like a snail
Digesting a garden, a green
Goods-train in a see-through tunnel.

Only after rain the pool
Shows its true colours. Tan
Bubbles rainbow and blink.
But then the hill
For all its granite bluff and spur
Has a vision of plains.

Pools cannot feed on air.

Landfall

It is coming up.
Where water beetles wheel on water
Over green depths like galaxies
Or dodgem cars, it is coming up.

The water-dragon stares as still
As the paperbark he lies along,
Fishing with his tongue.

The saucer comes up like a moon as if
The east had turned transparent and you saw
Below the glow of the horizon.

It is coming up a rope ladder
Of bubbles, waving claws,
Until its snake-head
Breaks the surface tension and
Two yellow eyes appraise the world of air.

The daylight moon
Crinkles in the pool
And beetles rock like dinghies.
The water-dragon does not stir.

Trim in his shell, the tortoise rows ashore.

Portents over Coffee

1.

Turtles hatch in the hot sands
of Florida. This summer
Shouldering from shells, they turned
Their backs on the nursery waters of the Gulf
And headed inland. Volunteers
Wheeling them to sea declare
Thousands slipped snake-headed through their hands
To perish on the highways.

2.

At Boston, Mass.
Five negro teenagers
Forced a young wife to drench herself
In gasolene, and flicked a match.
The woman in a hood of fire
Walked two crowded blocks and crossed
a street to call an ambulance.

3.

At the West Coast Sanctuary
For pelicans, at nesting time
The egg shells proved so frail
They smashed like unfired clay beneath
The feathers of the mother birds.
No young survived.

from *Two Songs with Spanish Burdens*

2. Spring Lambs

Winter blows itself out with quick cloud and white
    sunshine;
Crows go down the wind like crepe torn from a funeral
And their cry the tearing. You ride home in the evening
With a flame in one cheek and a lamb on your pommel.

If you feed my lambs, I shall kiss you;
Otherwise I'll feed them and you may kiss me.

Frost feathers the grass and furs the fence wires;
There's ice in the bucket and a moon in the morning
Over the paddocks where shadows are frozen
And you vanish in mist while I stand gazing.

If you feed my lambs, I shall kiss you;
Otherwise I'll feed them and you may kiss me.

White lambs leap up under the quince trees;
They suck blue milk from a dented bucket,
Tugging at my fingers and at my heart strings.
Thoughts follow your hoof tracks like a shy blue heeler.

If you feed my lambs, I shall kiss you;
Otherwise I'll feed them and you may kiss me.

Judith Wright (1915–   )

The Hawthorn Hedge

How long ago she planted the hawthorn hedge –
she forgets how long ago –
that barrier thorn across the hungry ridge;
thorn and snow.

It is twice as tall as the rider on the tall mare
who draws his reins to peer
in through the bee-hung blossom. Let him stare.
No one is here.

Only the mad old girl from the hut on the hill,
unkempt as an old tree.
She will hide away if you wave your hand or call;
she will not see.

Year-long, wind turns her grindstone heart and whets
a thornbranch like a knife,
shouting in winter 'Death'; and when the white bud sets,
more loudly, 'Life'.

She has forgotten when she planted the hawthorn hedge;
that thorn, that green, that snow;
birdsong and sun dazzled across the ridge –
it was long ago.

Her hands were strong in the earth, her glance on the sky,
her song was sweet on the wind.
The hawthorn hedge took root, grew wild and high
to hide behind.

Woman to Man

The eyeless labourer in the night,
the selfless, shapeless seed I hold,
builds for its resurrection day –
silent and swift and deep from sight
foresees the unimagined light.

This is no child with a child's face;
this has no name to name it by:
yet you and I have known it well.
This is our hunter and our chase,
the third who lay in our embrace.

This is the strength that your arm knows,
the arc of flesh that is my breast,
the precise crystals of our eyes.
This is the blood's wild tree that grows
the intricate and folded rose.

This is the maker and the made;
this is the question and reply;
the blind head butting at the dark,
the blaze of light along the blade.
Oh hold me, for I am afraid.

The Garden

Flowers of red silk and purple velvet grew
under the humming may-tree; the huge pines
made night across the grass, where the black snake
went whispering in its coils; and moving sunlight drew
copper fingers through the apple-trees.
Warm is the light the summer day refines,

and warm is she, whom life has made secure.
Walking slow along her garden ways,
a bee grown old at summer's end, she dips
and drinks that honey. All that we endure,
all that we meet and live through, gathers in our old age
and makes a shelter from the cold, she says.

Pulling around her shoulders her Joseph's-coat,
small bright bouquets reflected in her eyes,
this is the night's fit enemy and good friend
who has felt often his black hand at her throat;
and therefore my heart chose her, scarecrow, bag of old
    bones
Eve walking with her snake and butterfly.

Train Journey

Glassed with cold sleep and dazzled by the moon,
out of the confused hammering dark of the train
I looked and saw under the moon's cold sheet
your delicate dry breasts, country that built my heart;

and the small trees on their uncoloured slope
like poetry moved, articulate and sharp
and purposeful under the great dry flight of air,
under the crosswise currents of wind and star.

Clench down your strength, box-tree and ironbark.
Break with your violent root the virgin rock.
Draw from the flying dark its breath of dew
till the unliving come to life in you.

Be over the blind rock a skin of sense,
under the barren height a slender dance . . .

I woke and saw the dark small trees that burn
suddenly into flowers more lovely than the white moon.

Old House

Where now outside the weary house the pepperina,
that great broken tree, gropes with its blind hands
and sings a moment in the magpie's voice, there he stood
    once,
that redhaired man my great-great-grandfather,
his long face amiable as an animal's,
and thought of vines and horses.
He moved in that mindless country like a red ant,
running tireless in the summer heat among the trees –
the nameless trees, the sleeping soil, the original river –
and said that the eastern slope would do for a vineyard.

In the camp by the river they made up songs about him,
songs about the waggons, songs about the cattle,
songs about the horses and the children and the woman.
These were a dream, something strayed out of a dream.
They would vanish down the river, but the river would flow
    on,
under the river-oaks the river would flow on,
winter and summer would burn the grass white
or red like the red of the pale man's hair.
In the camp by the river they made up those songs
and my great-great-grandfather heard them with one part of
    his mind.

And in those days
there was one of him and a thousand of them,
and in these days none are left –
neither a pale man with kangaroo-grass hair
nor a camp of dark singers mocking by the river.
And the trees and the creatures, all of them are gone.
But the sad river, the silted river,
under its dark banks the river flows on,
the wind still blows and the river still flows.
And the great broken tree, the dying pepperina,
clutches in its hands the fragments of a song.

For Precision

Yet I go on from day to day, betraying
the core of light, the depth of darkness –
my speech inexact, the note not right,
never quite sure what I am saying –

on the periphery of truth. Uphold me now,
pure colours, blacks, whites, bells on the central tone,
middays, midnights. I wander among cross-lights.
Let me be sure and economical as the rayed
suns, stars, flowers, wheels: let me fall as a gull, a hawk

through the confusions of foggy talk,
and pin with one irremediable stroke –
what? – the escaping wavering wandering light,
the blur, the brilliance; forming into one chord
what's separate and distracted; making the vague hard –
catching the wraith – speaking with a pure voice,
and that the gull's sole note like a steel nail
that driven through cloud, sky, and irrelevant seas,
joins all, gives all a meaning, makes all whole.

The Curtain

It was the curtain, softly rising and falling,
reminded me you were home, who had been so long away;
and when I went to wake you, I stood in silence watching
your mouth softened in sleep, the lids where your eyes lay.

So grown you looked, in the same unaltered room,
so much of your childhood you were already forgetting,
while I remembered. Yet in the unforgetting dream
you will come here all your life for renewal and meeting.

It was your breath, so softly rising and falling,
that kept me silent. With your lids like buds unbroken
you watched on their curtain your life, a stream of shadows
    moving.
When I touched your shoulder, I too had a little dreamed
    and woken.

To Another Housewife

Do you remember how we went,
on duty bound, to feed the crowd
of hungry dogs your father kept
as rabbit-hunters? Lean and loud,
half-starved and furious, how they leapt
against their chains, as though they meant
in mindless rage for being fed,
to tear our childish hands instead!

With tomahawk and knife we hacked
the flyblown tatters of old meat,
gagged at their carcass-smell, and threw
the scraps and watched the hungry eat.
Then turning faint, we made a pact,
(two greensick girls), crossed hearts and swore
to touch no meat forever more.

How many cuts of choice and prime
our housewife hands have dressed since then –
these hands with love and blood imbrued –
for daughters, sons, and hungry men!
How many creatures bred for food
we've raised and fattened for the time
they met at last the steaming knife
that serves the feast of death-in-life!

And as the evening meal is served
we hear the turned-down radio
begin to tell the evening news
just as the family joint is carved.
O murder, famine, pious wars . . .
Our children shrink to see us so,
in sudden meditation, stand
with knife and fork in either hand.

Against the Wall

Knocking his knuckles against the wall
he watched the dust trickle awhile;
a scrap of glass from the mosaic,
the yellow robe of God the Father,
tinkled and fell. The floor's great flower
of tile and stone was cracked. A small
eye of light crossed choir and stall
and that great cave became archaic.
Surprised by this he knocked again.

He knocked again. Silently tilting
the great reredos tottered outward.
The antique wood, the stone uniquely
fashioned, all this by craftsmen finished,
unsigned except by Man, all perished
in one tall flourish of dust. And silting
the heaps of rubble, softly felting
the jags and edges, all fell meekly,
till a smooth hill awaited rain.

Knocking his knuckles against each other,
he sat and wept for rain to fall,
for tears and dust to breed together
the scarlet flower that saves us all –
the blood-red flower that saves us all.

Pro and Con

Death when he walks behind me frightens me –
soft-footed skulker in a darkened lane,
adept with silence, knives and treachery,
or the stunning blow, or chilly long indifference
that rots the heart and brain.

Death when I turn my head and see him there
meets me with a look I recognize.
Waking at birth to daylight's ruthless stare,
I cried for it, rebelled against enslaving sense
that opened my stung eyes.

Death whom I meet on main roads casually
turns a hairsbreadth wheel and waves goodbye.
By night we meet in old conspiracy
and conjugate 'to love' – past, present, future tense.
I wake, repeating 'I' –

'I' – 'I' – 'I' – the tuner testing one cracked note,
the child with one sore tooth.
Round rings of air melt outward from my throat,
bearing that lying truth.

Smalltown Dance

Two women find the square-root of a sheet.
That is an ancient dance:
arms wide: together: again: two forward steps: hands meet
your partner's once and twice.
That wide expanse
reduces to a neat
compression fitting in the smallest space
a sheet can pack in on a cupboard shelf.

High scented walls there were of flapping white
when I was small, myself.
I walked between them, playing Out of Sight.
Simpler than arms, they wrapped and comforted –
clean corridors of hiding, roofed with blue –
saying, Your sins too are made Monday-new;
and see, ahead
that glimpse of unobstructed waiting green.
Run, run before you're seen.

But women know the scale of possibility,
the limit of opportunity,
the fence,
how little chance
there is of getting out. The sheets that tug
sometimes struggle from the peg,
don't travel far. Might symbolise
something. Knowing where danger lies
you have to keep things orderly.
The household budget will not stretch to more.

And they can demonstrate it in a dance.
First pull those wallowing white dreamers down,
spread arms: then close them. Fold
those beckoning roads to some impossible world,
put them away and close the cupboard door.

from *For a Pastoral Family*

IV Pastoral Lives

Yet a marginal sort of grace
as I remember it, softened our arrogant clan.
We were fairly kind to horses
and to people not too different from ourselves.
Kipling and A. A. Milne were our favourite authors
but Shelley, Tennyson, Shakespeare stood on our shelves –
suitable reading for women,
to whom, after all, the amenities had to be left.

An undiscursive lot (discourse is for the city)
one of us helped to found a university.
We respected wit in others,
though we kept our own for weddings,
unsure of the bona fides of the witty.

In England, we called on relatives,
assuming welcome for the sake of a shared bloodline,
but kept our independence.
We would entertain them equally, if they came
and with equal hospitality –
blood being thicker than thousands of miles of waters –
for the sake of Great-aunt Charlotte and old letters.

At church, the truncate, inarticulate
Anglican half-confession
'there is no health in us'
made us gag a little. We knew we had no betters
though too many were worse.
We passed on the collection-plate
adding a reasonable donation.

That God approved us was obvious.
Most of our ventures were prosperous.
As for the *Dies Irae*
we would deal with that when we came to it.

VI Kinship

Blue early mist in the valley. Apricots
bowing the orchard trees, flushed red with summer,
loading bronze-plaqued branches;
our teeth in those sweet buttock-curves. Remember
the horses swinging to the yards, the smell
of cattle, sweat and saddle-leather?
Blue ranges underlined the sky. In any weather
it was well, being young and simple,
letting the horses canter home together.

All those sights, smells and sounds we shared
trailing behind grey sheep, red cattle,
from Two-rail or Ponds Creek
through tawny pastures breathing pennyroyal.
In winter, sleety winds bit hands and locked
fingers round reins. In spring, the wattle.

With so much past in common,
on the whole we forgive each other
for the ways in which we differ –
two old men, one older woman.
When one of us falls ill,
the others may think less
of today's person, the lined and guarding face,

than of a barefoot child running careless through
long grass where snakes lie, or forgetting
to watch in the paddocks for the black Jersey bull.
Divisions and gulfs deepen
daily, the world over
more dangerously than now between us three.
Which is why, while there is time (though not our form at
    all)
I put the memories into poetry.

James McAuley (1917–76)

Dialogue

There was a pattering in the rafters, mother,
My dreams were troubled by the sounds above.

– That is just a young man's fancy, son,
Lightly turning now to thoughts of love.

I heard things moving in the cellar, mother,
And once I thought that something touched my side.

– Your father used to hear those noises, son,
About the time that I became a bride.

And when I woke up in the cold dawn, mother,
The rats had come and eaten my face away.

– Never mind, my son, you'll get another,
Your father he had several in his day.

Jesus

Touching Ezekiel his workman's hand
Kindled the thick and thorny characters;
And seraphim that seemed a thousand eyes,
Flying leopards, wheels and basilisks,
Creatures of power and of judgment, soared
From his finger-point, emblazoning the skies.

Then turning from the book he rose and walked
Among the stones and beasts and flowers of earth;
They turned their muted faces to their Lord,
Their real faces, seen by God alone;
And people moved before him undisguised;
He thrust his speech among them like a sword.

And when a dove came to his hand he knew
That hell was opening behind its wings.
He thanked the messenger and let it go;
Spoke to the dust, the fishes and the twelve
As if they understood him equally,
And told them nothing that they wished to know.

from *The Hero and the Hydra*

IV The Tomb of Heracles

A dry tree with an empty honeycomb
Stands as a broken column by the tomb:
The classic anguish of a rigid fate,
The loveless will, superb and desolate.

This is the end of stoic pride and state:
Blind light, dry rock, a tree that does not bear.

Look, cranes still know their path through empty air;
For them their world is neither soon nor late;
But ours is eaten hollow with despair.

Father, Mother, Son

From the domed head the defeated eyes peer out,
Furtive with unsaid things of a lifetime, that now
Cannot be said by that stiff half-stricken mouth
Whose words come hoarse and slurred, though the mind is
    sound.

[88]

To have to be washed, and fed by hand, and turned
This way and that way by the cheerful nurses,
Who joke, and are sorry for him, and tired of him:
All that is not the worst paralysis.

For fifty years this one thread – he has held
One gold thread of the vesture: he has said
Hail, holy Queen, slightly wrong, each night in secret.
But his wife, and now a lifetime, stand between:

She guards him from his peace. Her love asks only
That in the end he must not seem to disown
Their terms of plighted troth. So he will make
For ever the same choice that he has made –

Unless that gold thread hold, invisibly.
I stand at the bed's foot, helpless like him;
Thinking of legendary Seth who made
A journey back to Paradise, to gain

The oil of mercy for his dying father.
But here three people smile, and, locked apart,
Prove by relatedness that cannot touch
Our sad geometry of family love.

Against the Dark

Life to be understood turns into legend:
    At last we recognize
The tales we always knew, of loss and finding;
    I read them in your eyes.

The impossible task is finished before cockcrow,
    The key turns in the door,
The withered garden flowers in the first springtime
    That no-one could restore.

For what we are can only be imagined;
    The story never lies:
It is our truthfulness in love it measures;
    I read it in your eyes.

One Tuesday in Summer

That sultry afternoon the world went strange.
Under a violet and leaden bruise
The air was filled with sinister yellow light;
Trees, houses, grass took on unnatural hues.

Thunder rolled near. The intensity grew and grew
Like doom itself with lightnings on its face.
And Mr Pitt, the grocer's order-man,
Who made his call on Tuesdays at our place,

Said to my mother, looking at the sky,
'You'd think the ending of the world had come.'
A leathern little man, with bicycle-clips
Around his ankles, doing our weekly sum,

He too looked strange in that uncanny light;
As in the Bible ordinary men
Turn out to be angelic messengers,
Pronouncing the Lord's judgments why and when.

I watched the scurry of the small black ants
That sensed the storm. What Mr Pitt had said
I didn't quite believe, or disbelieve;
But still the words had got into my head,

For nothing less seemed worthy of the scene.
The darkening imminence hung on and on,
Till suddenly, with lightning-stroke and rain,
Apocalypse exploded, and was gone.

By nightfall things had their familiar look.
But I had seen the world stand in dismay
Under the aspect of another meaning
That rain or time would hardly wash away.

Autumn in Hobart

Snow-cloud, a rainbow, blue sky, rain,
All at one time; the wet streets shine
In pale gold sunlight, a cold breeze ruffles
The reds and yellows of wet trees.
The yellow-throated honeyeater knows
How to like this place: he's active, greedy,
And defines his world with music.

Parish Church

Bonewhite the newborn flesh, the crucified,
The risen body; bonewhite the crowding faces.
Green, crimson, yellow, blue the robes are dyed,
The wings and armour, the skies and heavenly places.

We used to sing at Easter in the choir
With trumpet and harmonium and drums,
Feeling within our hearts new-kindled fire.
Now I'm the only one that ever comes.

I bring with me my griefs, my sins, my death,
And sink in silence as I try to pray.
Though in this calm no impulse stirs my breath,
At least there's nothing that I would unsay.

Anne Elder (1918–76)

Seen Out

> Some of them evil, most good,
> all nice people with various eyes.
> They are The Club.

The band has packed, the white cloths discreetly
being flapped and the dregs of the bubbly
drained in kitchens. The smoke
has been forced with the gaiety
up to the lofty ceiling; but some still sit
masticating the last rags of conversation.
The fine brain bends to its neighbouring dome, a frontal
obeisance as though to the Privy Council, sharing
dignity, reminiscence, a witticism
desiccated, deprecated. The beloved obstetrician
off duty is quacking softly
to an ex-victim. A shimmer, a trailed fur
looms in the archway, beckoning with a nose.
'Time, gentlemen, please . . . delightful . . . past our
    bed . . .'

In the hall they sort into a graceful procession,
here with a bluff arm or a blurry pleasantry,
here with the slightly inhibited belch of weary lechery,
there with even a touch of accustomed hands
as though in a decorous round-dance they have not needed
to rehearse for the last decade. Out into the night
through cedar portals they sway themselves.
The beautiful young wives, a little roguish and elated,
drop names, smoothing the satin laps of their success.
The great bosom beneath a purple coiffure
sinks with a constrained sigh into the front seat,
murmuring 'Shall I drive, dear?' Dear grunts.
They wheel their marriages on tyres to sleep,
calling it love. The party is over. They are paired.
Above all they are those who know how to behave.

Not a bad lot.
Most evils do some good –
as the hooked mullet
is stunned by a merciful club.

Crazy Woman

On the first day of autumn Euterpe called to me:
I am the Muse that sits musing under the lyric tree
plucking and plaiting the thoughtful branches
deep in the heart of the public gardens
where I first saw you, a queer child with your grandfather.
It is nice here, you should be with me.
We can sit alone.
I will pluck you and suck you the fruit for a serious poem.

So I went, and sure enough it was nice;
the first leaf already fallen,
the last white daisy still crawling
in bluish dewy grass, a pair of birds
black-white and neat, no longer matey, but still friendly,
unsurprised at my feet.
But another madwoman came by
and pecked me with her smile. Aren't they tame
she said, Yes I said, What's their name
she said, A couple called Magpie Lark I said,
built last spring, now semi-detached, it's autumn,
and she said fancy, what a shame.

I detached myself to the perfect seclusion
of the remembered grotto, the only intrusion
a fountaining cherubic boy, his little bronze spout
of Eros still delightful as when my grandfather
took pains not to point it out.
But a chap came by who was foreign.
You are zitting in vot beautiful zun, he said,
yes I said abstractedly (I was writing a serious poem)
and he went and sat tactfully
on the next seat. How lonely can you get
to be looking so slantingly
at my withering crossed knee.

For security I became engaged to the gardener
in passionately horticultural conversation
of considerable duration,
even to how the nights in the gardens of Spain
are enlivened with runnels and babbles
of conversational water, and he agreed with me
that the Spanish are gardeners of great subtlety.
What's that, I said, like a fern dotted with stars?
Oh that, that's a thing we've had for years
for which no municipal gardener cares,
but if you would like it, come into the shrubbery
and I will give you a good root
he said, with subtlety I thought,
and I jumped at it
and went off with my fern dripping good fruitful earth
down the mysterious path.

But along the misty vistas of Arcady
behold young lovers approaching, she
not beautiful but beautifully shy,
he with the true, the demented languishing eye,
swinging along wonderfully lonely
hand in hand worlds apart
by the width of the path
so that I met them where they joined, they dropped hands
for the Weird Woman gathering ferns and simples
and muttering God keep you under her breath
like a gipsy, meaning no harm.

I debated how to say it aloud,
to their alarm. Before our death
there is much to communicate that goes by the board
because it is thought unusual indeed crazy
to gather the fallen leaf and the daisy,
the magpie lark and the private lark
in the public park,
the eternal cherubic spout, the nakedness
and lovingness of loneliness
into the right word
to bless our other selves in the name of the Lord.

With coupled hands and crooked stare
and pointed smile they dance around
the poor old crazy head-in-air,
the poet, who has first to find
the spangled fern, the gift, then grow it
bedded in the heart's ground.

Yarra Park

The Park at the arse end of Winter
gets the wind. Can springs be far behind
the seedy preambles of these raddled lovers
parked, empty can chucked out,
transported by transistor, an erect
clutch in the way?

Can ever Spring come sweetly? Once
to the old coppice of tented oaks, once
to the billabong where the wild quinces
and mulberries remember a farm.
Disgust scums the water, the oak leaves crackle
on smashed vicious glass.

Once is long ago. Kids are born
strident in gangs from a concrete school,
straggle and are gone to farting buses.
Park. To the wind my great shining
red dog running roundly, the beauty
running . . .

Good evening, my river between willows moving;
run, in the dark, from the stains on the papers.
In my once house I make arsenic tea
for all despoilers, stick
my rat-eyed head in a bag of rags
and nest restless with my mate, hate;
and the Spring will be borne.

This parish was Warringal
for 'wild dog jumping quickly'.
And before that in the valley
they roamed the Yarra Yarra,
the white bark arching over.
The tribe was Jika Jika.
They walked in pride for ever.

Singers of Renown

I listen each week to the discs
on radio, superlative voices
busting their boilers to bring us
nostalgia. Being a woman, it is the tenors
and baritones who afford me
most mellifluous pain
at the heart. Standing tonight at the door
I took over evening fields and listen
to someone's immortal heartache.
                          What more
can I do but watch an eagle wheeling
into night and write
this dry little verse, collapsing
the whole sexuality of men and women
via the voice into one ragged stanza.

Still, it is done, and I can go to the kitchen
having loved my little bit with a pen
and unaccompanied. Catharsis
makes bearable the frying of brains.
I thank you,
plump amorous tenor, I thank you
with tender stewed plums.

To a Friend under Sentence of Death

In about a week, they say
you will be gone.
It is valuable time.
I walk slowly about this town.
The heartbeat seems to have shifted somewhat
to dead centre under the breastbone
swinging the weight of a clock.
Displacements are unnatural.
So is the total disappearance of my car.

With perfect naturalness I walk about
making no enquiries, simply
pursuing whereabouts
in the grid of streets and meeting
with perfect naturalness Walter Mitty
round every next corner, hailing him gaily
for coffee, a cigarette, and what
in God's name to talk about,
to walk about, walk off
the map, to be better off without,
inwardly shaking, knowing you still
lying in this town. In about a week
they say blandly
who are not acquainted with death
on a week's rope
weight of a clock . . .

Gwen Harwood (1920–   )

Prize-Giving

Professor Eisenbart, asked to attend
a girls' school speech night as an honoured guest
and give the prizes out, rudely declined;
but from indifference agreed, when pressed
with dry scholastic jokes, to change his mind,
to grace their humble platform, and to lend

distinction (of a kind not specified)
to the occasion. Academic dress
became him, as he knew. When he appeared
the girls whirred with an insect nervousness,
the Head in humbler black flapped round and steered
her guest, superb in silk and fur, with pride

to the best seat beneath half-hearted blooms
tortured to form the school's elaborate crest.
Eisenbart scowled with violent distaste,
then recomposed his features to their best
advantage: deep in thought, with one hand placed
like Rodin's Thinker. So he watched the room's

mosaic of young heads. Blonde, black, mouse-brown
they bent for their Headmistress' opening prayer.
But underneath a light (no accident
of seating, he felt sure), with titian hair
one girl sat grinning at him, her hand bent
under her chin in mockery of his own.

Speeches were made and prizes given. He shook
indifferently a host of virgin hands.
'*Music!*' The girl with titian hair stood up,
hitched at a stocking, winked at nearby friends,
and stood before him to receive a cup
of silver chased with curious harps. He took

her hand, and felt its voltage fling his hold
from his calm age and power; suffered her strange
eyes, against reason dark, to take his stare
with her to the piano, there to change
her casual schoolgirl's for a master's air.
He forged his rose-hot dream as Mozart told

the fullness of all passion or despair
summoned by arrogant hands. The music ended,
Eisenbart teased his gown while others clapped,
and peered into a trophy which suspended
his image upside down: a sage fool trapped
by music in a copper net of hair.

Boundary Conditions

'At the sun's incredible centre
    the atomic nuclei
with electrons and light quanta
    in a burning concord lie.
All the particles that form
    light and matter, in that furnace
keep their equilibrium.
    Once we pass beyond the surface
of the star, sharp changes come.
    These remarks apply as well
to the exploding atom bomb,'
    said Professor Eisenbart
while his mistress, with a shell
    scored an arrow and a heart
in the sand on which they lay
    watching heat and light depart
from the boundaries of day.

'Sprung from love's mysterious core
   soul and flesh,' the young girl said,
'restless on the narrow shore
   between the unborn and the dead,
split from concord, and inherit
   mankind's old dichotomy:
mind and matter; flesh and spirit;
   what has been and what will be;
desire that flares beyond our fate:
   still in the heart more violence lies
than in the bomb. Who'll calculate
   that tough muscle's bursting size?'

Tongues of darkness licked the crust
   of pigment from the bowl of blue.
Thought's campaniles fell to dust
   blown by the seawind through and through.

In the Park

She sits in the park. Her clothes are out of date.
Two children whine and bicker, tug her skirt.
A third draws aimless patterns in the dirt.
Someone she loved once passes by – too late

to feign indifference to that casual nod.
'How nice,' et cetera. 'Time holds great surprises.'
From his neat head unquestionably rises
a small balloon . . . 'but for the grace of God . . .'

They stand a while in flickering light, rehearsing
the children's names and birthdays. 'It's so sweet
to hear their chatter, watch them grow and thrive,'
she says to his departing smile. Then, nursing
the youngest child, sits staring at her feet.
To the wind she says, 'They have eaten me alive.'

Person to Person

So we meet as of old where the rosevine
is tied to a trellis with rags, and the flowers
push us left to that place we know; now the town
with its murmuring ceaseless invention
of old, friendly ghosts among tree-clustered greens
lies quiet below.

I speak of those years when I lived
walled alive in myself, left with nothing
but the inward search for joy, for a word
that would ruffle the plumage of mind to reach
its tenderest down; when consuming
myself I endured, but could not change.

Through the rents in a wall the fresh weeds
are labouring for sunlight.
                              This perfect joy
excludes any feeling of joy, and we laugh
at the world and its crazy perspectives,
at the suburbs' impotent trimmings
and guilt-driven labour,

and talk, with a deeper passion
than delight in our skill.
                              I reach to take
your hand, and a thorn from the rosevine
rakes blood from my wrist.
                              I cannot hear
what you say as a child comes to wake me
by scraping his nails on my arm.

Who grows old in a dream, who can taste
the ripe wholeness of absence? And who can summon
by light the incredible likeness of sleep?
From this fading dream as useless now
as a torn-off wing I wake to embrace
the stubborn presence of life.

Dust to Dust

I dream I stand once more
in Ann Street by the old
fire station. The palms
like feather dusters move
idly in stifling air.
The sky's dusted with gold.
A footfall; someone comes;
I cannot speak for love.

We walk in silence past
All Saints'. The dead do rise,
do live, do walk and wear
their flesh. Your exile's done.
So, so, resume our last
rejoicing kiss. Your eyes
flecked with my image stare
in wonder through my own.

Round us air turns to flame.
Ashes rain from the sky.
A firebell clangs and clangs
insanely as I wake
to absence with your name
shaping my lips. I lie
losing the dream that hangs
fading in air. I shake

the last of night away.
These bright motes that define
morning inside my room
hold not one grain of you.
Another sunstruck day
whose moving dust-motes shine
remote from any dream
cannot restore, renew

our laughter that hot night
when by All Saints' we talked
in the brief time we had.
During *Magnificat*
an urchin stopped to write
on the church wall. He chalked
his message: GOD IS MAD.
I say amen to that.

Winter Quarters

We sit in someone else's house
a-drinking at the dry red wine
after long separation, flaunting
banners of memory with their strange
devices (others watching us
for intimations of some fine
poetic love-death) round the haunting
sense of a time no time can change.

We learn from one involving stare
all men are mortal, and we are
human indeed. The triumphs won
from time remain invisible.
Years, that have taught us how to wear
defeat like an old duelling scar
paled to distinction, flash and run
like minutes to this beautiful

half-drunken *now*, where we might be
two captains resting, wearied by
a long campaign, at ease yet still
alert, friends long enough to show
the heart's true gentleness, to see
the mask of day's authority
put by, drinking night's peace until
a word, a look, can say: I know

as I am known. I look. I store
the memory that must serve so long.
Feature by feature I record
your ageing face, through which the loved
unageing spirit shines once more
to liberate the pulse of song
in that calm centre where each word
hangs like a waterdrop unmoved

in early quietness, the real
presence of morning globed in light.
Look long and truthfully. Each scar
declares our living worth. Be sure
that the clean wounds of time will heal.
Rejoice in this unwounded night.
The young are beautiful. We are
ourselves, and love, and will endure.

Looking towards Bruny

In a hollow where late-mown pasture lapses to straw
a flower not the colour of any flower
blows open and shut in gentle air.
Black calyx, blood-black corolla,
and filaments of sinew:
some creature has eaten crow
and liked it.
                    What prospect has the eye?
The low hills of Bruny rise
to a silver-grey wash of cloud.
A hectoring flight of crows
descending like torn-up shadows
enters a pine-tree's singular darkness.
The ferry *Mangana* draws
in its wake a friction of lights
across the steel-shining channel
        where Truganini was held
        in a rowboat by two white sawyers

whose hatchets crunched on black wrists
as her drowning companions clutched the gunwale.
She suffers that fourfold wound.
Four bodiless hands surrender
the snapping derision of bones
to the solid mercy of water.
While history suckles the race
who ride the *Mangana* to Bruny
to brown their winter-pale skins
sea-monsters draw out the breast
in secret currents black fingers open and close.

Dialogue

If an angel came with one wish
I might say, deliver that child
who died before birth, into life.
Let me see what she might have become.
He would bring her into a room
fair-skinned   the bones of her hands
would press on my shoulderblades
in our long embrace
                                    we would sit
with the albums spread on our knees:
now here are your brothers   and here
your sister   here the old house
among trees and espaliered almonds.
   – But where am I?
                                    Ah my dear
I have only one picture
                                    here
in my head   I saw you lying
still folded   one moment   forever
your head bent down to your heart
eyes closed on unspeakable wisdom
your delicate frog-pale fingers
                                    spread

apart as if you were playing
a woodwind instrument.
   – My name?
            It was never given.
   – Where is my grave?
            in my head   I suppose
the hospital burnt you.
   – Was I beautiful?
            To me.
   – Do you mourn for me every day?
Not at all   it is more than thirty years
I am feeling the coolness of age
the perspectives of memory change.
Pearlskull   what lifts you here
from night-drift to solemn ripeness?
Mushroom dome? Gourd plumpness?
The frog in my pot of basil?
   – It is none of these, but a rhythm
     the bones of my fingers   dactylic
     rhetoric smashed from your memory.
     Forget me again
                 Had I lived
     no rhythm would be the same
     nor my brothers and sister feast
     in the world's eternal house.

Overhead   wings of cloud
     burning   and under my feet
        stones marked with demons' teeth.

Mother Who Gave Me Life

Mother who gave me life
I think of women bearing
women. Forgive me the wisdom
I would not learn from you.

It is not for my children I walk
on earth in the light of the living.
It is for you, for the wild
daughters becoming women,

anguish of seasons burning
backward in time to those other
bodies, your mother, and hers
and beyond, speech growing stranger

on thresholds of ice, rock, fire,
bones changing, heads inclining
to monkey bosom, lemur breast,
guileless milk of the word.

I prayed you would live to see
Halley's Comet a second time.
The Sister said, When she died
she was folding a little towel.

You left the world so, having lived
nearly thirty thousand days:
a fabric of marvels folded
down to a little space.

At our last meeting I closed
the ward door of heavy glass
between us, and saw your face
crumple, fine threadbare linen

worn, still good to the last,
then, somehow, smooth to a smile
so I should not see your tears.
Anguish: remembered hours:

a lamp on embroidered linen,
my supper set out, your voice
calling me in as darkness
falls on my father's house.

Rosemary Dobson (1920–   )

from *Daily Living*

3. Visiting

The stick, the fan, the basket, the morning paper,
But first the task – hymn-books to be gathered
After the morning service. There's an old girl playing

'Jealousy' from sheet-music at the piano,
('I make my fingers work. It's the arthritis.')
I walk with my mother outside round the garden.

Some rage simmers in all of us all the time.
I know her rage as mine. 'Oh, these
Old women –' she says, as though a mutinous girl,

Who all her life has so compliantly
Deferred to accident, event, and time.
Something behind the drained blue of her eyes

Flashes. We go inside and gather up
The basket, stick, and fan, and the unread
News of another world. We say goodbye.

Daily I leave so and am glad to go.
Daily she tells me of her troubled dreams.
I listen. Could not bear to tell her mine.

5. Folding the Sheets

You and I will fold the sheets
Advancing towards each other
From Burma, from Lapland,

From India where the sheets have been washed in the river
And pounded upon stones:
Together we will match the corners.

From China where women on either side of the river
Have washed their pale cloth in the White Stone Shallows
'Under the shining moon'.

We meet as though in the formal steps of a dance
To fold the sheets together, put them to air
In wind, in sun over bushes, or by the fire.

We stretch and pull from one side and then the other –
Your turn. Now mine.
We fold them and put them away until they are needed.

A wish for all people when they lie down in bed –
Smooth linen, cool cotton, the fragrance and stir of herbs
And the faint but perceptible scent of sweet clear water.

Dimitris Tsaloumas (1921–   )

An Extravagant Lover's Note of Explanation

Sitting on the divan
with knees drawn up
and sipping wine as if
to quench a great thirst
between word and word,
you may have thought
my welcome inadequate
after so long.

What happened in fact
is that the rain had stopped
and left me numb
and all the pens had stopped
their dripping too
over the wide world where maids
came out of every door
with mops to scrub it clean

and clear. And so the cat
he walked straight out
of coiled gloom and sprang
on to the sill
tail in the twitching air,
my gold coins found holes
and started rolling
to the nearest charity box
and from the window right
behind you I saw my shirt
crossing the road
with St Vincent de Paul
and a great shaft of light
pour down from a rose-window
over Port Phillip Bay
where a tanker's poop stood tall

in it, like the archangel
in Jan Van Eyck's
Annunciation. This,

and the Festival of Rockets.
Because our nuclear warheads
left their silos and flew
into the air across the sky
festive and stainless bright
with patriotic markings
brighter than Sunday kites
on Elwood beach,
and they flew with streamers
and fairwell flags
over the cheering crowds
and then streaked off
all in the same direction
and through the gap
above the Pole they vanished
into the darkest hole

man ever dug. And I thought
I'd tell you. Ruffled cushions,
two empty bottles and ashes
scattered about the floor
sum up but a presence
of hours. Yet it has changed
immutable things.
My pictures hang all excited
on furbished hooks,
a batting of the eyelid here
and there a stirring of leaves.
Springtime paper covers
the cracking walls,
on coffee tables grim texts
gape gay with colour
in glossy editions. Also,
the cistern now works,
the dingy kitchen's light

with polished lino and sparkl-
ing sink. Of course
these renovations mightn't be
what you'd expect. Nevertheless,
I thought I'd let you know.

The Grudge

Strange that your image should occur to me
as I beat the grass for snakes in this

forsaken patch. It doesn't seem right to me.
I have always thought your manner somewhat

too correct, but your business dealings
are of good report. Or is it the woman

who shares my bed? She burns in the flesh
of many a man and I find it galling, I confess,

that you should never look at her that way.
It kind of blunts the sting of my pleasure.

Nor does the splendour of my house and fame
move you much. Yet there you are, my friend,

flushed out of grass by the scouting stick
amid the knotted vines, pleasant as ever,

tall in the haze a cut above the likes of me.
It bothers me. This is my brother's vineyard.

Alexander Craig (1923–)

The Ceiling

Green sweater a little rubbed
thin hair uncut and yellow.
Poised as it seems,
observing carefully,

'Loathe him,' she says. But almost every night
after the evening lecture, drinking talking
in the Town House bistro with boys
her own age, still she leaves with him
or, if he works at home, will steal away
to tap on the door of the downstairs flat.

Always he condescends, demonstrating
again the things he's taught her. Lastly his back
curves like a shell beneath the bedclothes breath
wheezing asthmatically in sleep. But she
lying too long awake stares at an unlit lighthouse:

it's upside-down in a gently undulating
grey ceiling. Bewilderment
could easily bring tears, but frowning
she reaches up into the rippled shadow
for nothing she knows.

from *Sea Change*

VII The Bottles

No longer glimpsing a few beer cans that glint
in ruts or under a clump of bushes
you notice along the ground beside the tyre tracks

a trail of tall brown bottles
They stand or lean or lie
filtering the light
Maybe you're staring right down
at the small round mouths
still open in glassy wonder

or backing away and seeing the necks turn into fingers
to point at the sky or horizontally
argue for different directions

When the sun has climbed steeply into a bare sky
and when no grassblade stirs
no tree tilts in a great wind
no branch is braced for birdclaw

they dazzle the eyes whose dark lustre shows
how you thirst for a shining coolness not contained by glass
not held by metal to mock your hunger

Francis Webb (1925–73)

The Day of the Statue

You look for prodigies leaning on the sill of storm,
Or loose in the yellow gap at a candle's end,
But here was patience: fishermen out on the bay,
Work and silence inching with the minute-hand.

Moored in a lulled spinny of sun and shadow,
With an impotent tremor in the sails, the ketch nosed down
To the long lunge of the swell, rose dripping, gasping
As if with eagerness to suck in air again.

And the men, snug in this casual pediment of time,
Their gestures grouped and restricted and interlocking,
Felt the haul stubborn to their hands, and eye-tooth
    wrenched
From the iron gums of the sea-bed, shuddering and aching.

As it cleared the surface, green sinews of water
Dangled and fell away. With the bursting of cords
Something strained at the trap of its dissolution,
Dull centuries of pressure and lust of weeds.

A bronze youth, moulded as a lyric or a prayer
But mocked by the sea, deformed in his grey sheet,
Sprawled like a scar on the mottled flesh of planks
While his finders cursed at the torn strings of their net.

There were some to roll back the heavy stone of the sea;
There was none to ponder the mortal, the living token.
But later, men polished, incised, established at last
What that raised hand once clutched and years had broken.

Morgan's Country

This is Morgan's country: now steady, Bill.
(Stunted and grey, hunted and murderous.)
Squeeze for the first pressure. Shoot to kill.

Five: a star dozing in its cold cavern.
Six: first shuffle of boards in the cold house.
And the sun lagging on seven.

The grey wolf at his breakfast. He cannot think
Why he must make haste, unless because their eyes
Are poison at every well where he might drink.

Unless because their gabbling voices force
The doors of his grandeur – first terror, then only hate.
Now terror again. Dust swarms under the doors.

Ashes drift on the dead-sea shadow of his plate.
Why should he heed them? What to do but kill
When his angel howls, when the sounds reverberate

In the last grey pipe of his brain? At the window sill
A blowfly strums on two strings of air:
Ambush and slaughter tingle against the lull.

But the Cave, his mother, is close beside his chair,
Her sunless face scribbled with cobwebs, bones
Rattling in her throat when she speaks. And there

The stone Look-out, his towering father, leans
Like a splinter from the seamed palm of the plain.
Their counsel of thunder arms him. A threat of rain.

Seven: and a blaze fiercer than the sun.
The wind struggles in the arms of the starved tree,
The temple breaks on a threadbare mat of glass.

Eight: even under the sun's trajectory
This country looks grey, hunted and murderous.

For My Grandfather

When the ropes droop and loosen, and the gust
Piecemeal upon a widening quietness fails,
Fail breath and spirit; against the bony mast
Work in like skin the frayed and slackened sails.
In the green lull where ribs and keel lie wrecked,
Wrapped in the sodden, enigmatic sand,
Things that ache sunward, seaward, with him locked,
Tug at the rigging of the dead ship-lover's hand.
Though no wind's whitening eloquence may fill
Drowned canvas with the steady bulge of breath,
Doubling for past, for future, are never still
The bones ambiguous with life and death.

Dusk over Bradley's Head: a feeble gull
Whose sinking body is the past at edge
Of form and nothing; here the beautiful
Letona gybes, off the spray-shaken ledge.
And to those years dusk comes but as a rift
In the flesh of sunlight, closed by memory;
Shells stir in the pull of water, lift
Fragile and holy faces to the sky.
My years and yours are scrawled upon this air
Rapped by the gavel of my living breath:
Rather than time upon my wrist I wear
The dial, the four quarters, of your death.

The Gunner

When the gunner spoke in his sleep the hut was still,
Uneasily strapped to the reckless wheel of his will;
Silence, humble, directionless as fog,
Lifted, and minutes were rhythmical on the log;

While slipstream plucked at a wafer of glass and steel,
Engines sliced and scooped at the air's thin wall,
And those dim spars dislodged from the moon became
Red thongs of tracer whipping boards aflame.

Listening, you crouched in the turret, watchful and taut
– *Bogey two thousand, skipper, corkscrew to port* –
Marvellous, the voice: driving electric fires
Through the panel of sleep, the black plugs, trailing wires.

The world spoke through its dream, being deaf and blind,
Its words were those of the dream, yet you might find
Forgotten genius, control, alive in this deep
Instinctive resistance to the perils of sleep.

Dawn Wind on the Islands

The needle of dawn has drugged them, life and death,
Stiff and archaic, mouldering into one,
Voiceless, having no mission and no path,
Lolling under a heavy head-dress. When
The puppet sun jerks up, there will be no
Convergences: the dead will be the dead,
Twirled in a yellow eddy, frail and dull.
These hands of mine that might be stone and snow,
Half bone, half silent fallen dust, will shed
Decay, and flower with the first glittering gull.

Dawn on the wide deserted airstrip swells
And the wind shifts and gains and gathers. If
The point of daylight balances, controls
The sense of life-and-death as on a gaff,
Then dripping it will come, and living – show
From this sea's knotted blue that has no name
While the moon dies on its branches like a leaf;
As coral's whitening belly it will flow
Inland before the sunrise, hang with flame
The tilted freighter breaking on the reef.

Here, where they died, oblivion will burn
The moth-winged bomber's glass and gristle; weirs
Of time will burst, burying them; the sun
Casually mock a cross of stars.
And I have watched them die, wedged fast, below
The tumbling barracks and the yellowing page,
Each day more helpless and more desperate.
At dawn these agonies break loose and grow
Out of the rotted boards, the voices rage:
Cry, cry, but feel – but never forget.

The sun will rise, and with its landward swing
The dead will be the dead, surrendered up
To a dark annexation. Life will hang
Red lights of warning on the crumbling ship.
There will be only life and death. The slow
Roll of the east, the passport of the day
Blazing release, while still this moment lies
Over the island, this. I cannot know
If it is life that wakes, shaking the bay,
Hungry, and circling, and labouring to rise.

Vlamingh and Rottnest Island

Christmas – always, forever, a Morning and a Coming.
Dawn is that village of the north
Casting its net of snow for our home-thought;
Or dawn is groggy Batavia's transforming,
Perhaps the rumour, venture of an actual light
In the huzzahs and the haze of our setting-forth.

Christmas and three ships, token of far places.
The sea-grain's fruitless fastening
On our numb timbers, all the sea like a stylus
With its bickering passport-motion at our faces.
Magi of a kind? for the Company's divine remoteness
Launched us, their yellow bunting above us listening.

Christmas, past dawn. It is not the Ridderschap Van
    Holland
(Errant star of our search) that is born on water,
Shepherded by coarse cloud with an eastern smile.
But with gulls galore it bears itself well, this island,
As a small craft, and every fulfilling mile
Brings closer to us some newborn navigator.

Face to face. Midday. He deals us the black swan's
Dive of welcome from shingle to promontory,
His queer-shaped trees have the reassuring leaf,
His smoke is the penmanship of a man's hands,
And lastly he opens the tattered log of the reef:
Fallen kings, wreckage – but never a word of our quarry.

Towards the Land of the Composer

Rain tries the one small foot and at length the other
On the tin roof.
Valves of my cheap set
Manage your name after some notes on the weather.

And we must all be moving, with all our baggage:
Icon of knobby tree,
Kouros of long-tailed animal,
Lepidoptera,
River Yarra,
Harbour Bridge,
Four-letter words, and tons of more personal luggage.

And the best fire of 'em all, made of mallee-roots,
Must stop this breezy nonsense,
Pull itself together
To run red and straight, after the swagman's boots.

And fair in the heel of the hunt our cloud-formations,
Our sun,
Our flocks,
Our tribespeople,
Grease of desert,
Blazing skewer of harvest,
The statues of Colonel Light, and the railway-stations.

And the heaven-bent squatters lash to their holy backs
Acre and acre,
Rifle and rifle,
The Family Tree,
The Family Bible,
At a sign from deadbeaters who carry only their packs.

And never a word nor a squeak from us when we meet
All the new islands,
All the old temples,
All the strange accents:
For the Leader has just this moment taken his seat.

And the latecoming bearded fish, and the smack and her
    crew,
Man-eating headlands,
Crystal women,
Sagas of ice,
Front-seat fjords,
Whirling noiselessly in to be close to you.

A Death at Winson Green

There is a green spell stolen from Birmingham;
Your peering omnibus overlooks the fence,
Or the grey, bobbing lifelines of a tram.
Here, through the small hours, sings our innocence.
Joists, apathetic pillars plot this ward,
Tired timbers wheeze and settle into dust,
We labour, labour: for the treacherous lord
Of time, the dazed historic sunlight, must
Be wheeled in a seizure towards one gaping bed,
Quake like foam on the lip, or lie still as the dead.

Visitors' Day: the graven perpetual smile,
String-bags agape, and pity's laundered glove.
The last of the heathens shuffles down the aisle,
Dark glass to a beauty which we hate and love.
Our empires rouse against this ancient fear,
Longsufferings, anecdotes, levelled at our doom;
Mine-tracks of old allegiance, prying here,
Perplex the sick man raving in his room.
Outside, a shunting engine hales from bed
The reminiscent feast-day, long since dead.

Noon reddens, trader birds deal cannily
With Winson Green, and the slouch-hatted sun
Gapes at windows netted in wire, and we
Like early kings with book and word cast down
Realities from our squared electric shore.
Two orderlies are whistling-in the spring;
Doors slam; and a man is dying at the core
Of triumph won. As a tattered, powerful wing
The screen bears out his face against the bed,
Silver, derelict, rapt, and almost dead.

Evening gropes out of colour; yet we work
To cleanse our shore from limpet histories;
Traffic and factory-whistle turn berserk;
Inviolate, faithful as a saint he lies.
Twilight itself breaks up, the venal ship,
Upon the silver integrity of his face.
No bread shall tempt that fine, tormented lip.
Let shadow switch to light – he holds his place.
Unmarked, unmoving, from the gaping bed
Towards birth he labours, honour, almost dead.

The wiry cricket moiling at his loom
Debates a themeless project with dour night,
The sick man raves beside me in his room;
I sleep as a child, rouse up as a child might.
I cannot pray; that fine lip prays for me
With every gasp at breath; his burden grows
Heavier as all earth lightens, and all sea.
Time crouches, watching, near his face of snows.
He is all life, thrown on the gaping bed,
Blind, silent, in a trance, and shortly, dead.

Nessun Dorma

in memory of Jussi Bjorling

Past six o'clock. I have prayed. No one is sleeping.
I have wandered past the old maternity home's
Red stone fermented by centuries; and there comes
New light, new light; and the cries of the rooks sweeping
To their great nests are guerilla light in a fusion
– Murmurs, echoes, plainsong; and the night
Will be all an abyss and depth of light between
Two shorelines in labour: birth and death. O passion
(One light in the hospital window) of quickening light,
O foetus quaking towards light, sound the gaunt green,
Trawl Norfolk, and make shiver the window-blind,
Harass nebulae for Bjorling. Find him, find.

And now the bar, the feeble light, glissade
Of tables and glasses, and the mantel-set
Intoning his death. Broad tender sunlights fret
Our twilight, his remembered voice has laid
Cock-crow and noon upon harrowed palms of the sill.
O broad light and tender, lucent aria,
Lacerate my paling cheeklines with the steep
Bequest of light and tears, flood me until
The man is the dawning child; be anathema
To man-made darkness. No one, no one shall sleep
Till the cry of the infant emergent, lost and lame,
Is the cry of a death gone towering towards the Flame.

Vincent Buckley (1925–88)

Death in January

Often, among the night-sounds, I've heard
Sound of the sea melting. Now, in mid-heat,
It's a striding coolness towards the palped sand,
Level enough to be stalked or ridden,
Thick green, topiary darkness
Fretting out to combings, wash, froth,
Paradise entering all paradises.

Some men work intrigues, some poems.
A spider working his cobweb in the dunes
Keeps his paranoiac watch on the sea,
Unnerved by water. The couples lie,
Foot-soles stretched to it,
Arms straightened, mouths slightly open,
Careful throats, ochreous muscles.
Native to water, yet afraid
Of blood. The sea-breeze
Rocks rocks in the transistor's head.
You couldn't surf in this.
And somehow the browned flesh feels not so doomed.

Later, the soft fume of delaying sun
Will be mist and light together
On the doused fire of waves
Where the few swimmers' peewit voices
Drift over like echoes of their bodies.

Disregarding them, some girl
With a child's head and enormous hat
And white nose of a clown will go on lying,
No longer warmed, but hardly noticing,
Offering her throat to the wind.

from *Golden Builders*

III Practising not Dying (i)

Even if there'd been prayers
Left for an hour, not quite prayed,
Hanging like chill strings in the air,
You'd have no choice

You'd have to lie back, trying
Vaguely for a normal
Pulse. One knee crooked on the other
As if no more could happen

To you, already stone, with a limewhite
Skin – your mouth
An unslaked taste. Waiting, knowing
Anything can happen.

The rasp of water running somewhere.
You go to splash it on your face
Coils of browned tap-thick water
Settle over your hands. You don't

Dry them, you lie back again.
Two or three small house-flies
Settle, flaying at your mouth.
Your hand bumps on your cheekbone

As you go to flick them off.

If you lie long enough
Who knows what will settle
On your face or hand: a shredded
Fragment of carbon

Drifted through the window, a globule
Of hot weld,
A dried morsel of cypress,
A seed from the uprooted spiky bush.

XIX

How soon will some self-turning
find me caught
in that ultimate stance of the poet,
the Montale watcher-figure,
brown-faced, cinematic,
half-hidden in the salt air,
hands bent in his pockets.

Shall I at will recall you

as you went past me
the hair moved on your shoulders
the straight waist hardly walking

bring you to mind
as you stand   and you are one line
from nape to ankle
your foot pivots
a dancer's movement on the stone.

Shall I catch back
the bobble of fuchsia-red
that almost touched you
swings now once or twice   and you stand
keeping its movement in you
        as in the soundproof room
        you begin to hear
        the still air flowing

It should be hot today
the sun quivering
the wind flat on the magnolia,
every ounce of the earth rising

XXl

The rain gusts at the asphalt
rhythm by rhythm, weightless as sleep,
all surfaces stripped cold

   bone city
streets like drains/like rust corrode you/the street lamps/
saltlight aureole/shines gapped houses. I
fighting my consciousness

    I dread these streets

flick flick the shadows go
vibrating in the clear space
of sunlight   and the cars endlessly
with a stripped sound
on paced macadam
    I dread them
pale concrete/sleds through them/swerving slowly through
 space

the long cough/of crushed cities
they blind me/ they respect nothing
so little air/ left, the centre is displaced
two bodies where one could live/ each face
heavy with damp

    Driven through it,
I turned in my seat-belt as the driver said
'the city's clear today'. But
over the bridge Vickers-Ruwolt
mashing out its lengthening
masks of smoke
sulphurous Brueghel-red swirlings in air.

Clear city.

Clear as flute and bells. Mouth-organ music.

Along the boulevard it sings; down thrawn alleys
shifts out like grass-smoke
past the weak doors of Dorrit St.
Human mouths   record players
O their monotonous cool teaches me
to see static, hear curving space.

The Blind School

rasps with crying. All night,
the corridor and side verandah
spark with lights, over the wet grass,
as voice after voice cry
without aim, gulping unseen air.

Chunky, round-eyed, neat, held
softly in my arms,
burrowing your face against me
you cry out, rasping, not to come
past me to the wastes of sleep.

They come past me in the street,
yoked in groups; pale heads
like a worm's, struggling,
feeling out the way,
they pat with their hands, their feet
loll over paving-cracks. They echo,
laughing, with the thought of laughter.

Your head rests in my shoulder.
Under your soft scalp the brain
beats, running like a heart; you tremble
as if, from off my skin, thick
spume, blood, mouse-matter
fled into your dreams.

Cicadas steam at the earth
under the blind school; behind
the gauzy wire there are gusts of shrilling.
In the clear space of your parents' bed you
sob with closed eyes, your voice a flashlight
ebbing in the dark around me.

'In the famine years Schull
was a place of skeletons.'
They sat propped in the streets,
each cabin inside its bawn
of spit and blood-clotted faeces.
'Skibbereen also was a famine centre.'
'There, in a parish of 18,000,
there were fifty deaths every day.'
'The cornstore at Durrus was filled with children.'
All were dying. 'Look there, Sir, you cannot
tell whether they are boys or girls.'
'Their legs swing and rock like
the legs of a doll . . . Sir, they have
the smell of mice.' 'Every one of them
is in famine fever, a fever
so sticky it never leaves them.'

Dying to sleep,
not knowing how to begin
that slow climb down, you
hold my clock on the pillow,
its gold-black face,
its hands sticking on twelve

And you burrow back, down
towards the unimaginable centre,
angrily 'Mamma, Mamma' (whose hair
is moving in the glistenings of street light).

Your Father's House

No place was like your father's house. I followed
you round and round, grinning,
nervy with your pleasure; even when,
bedded down, fatigued with ancestry,
kneeing the blankets, I heard their
soft laughter rustling the kitchen
and over the orchard's dung smells
the apple-trees made their furred sound
of green moving
                       it was as though
I lay along the buds
of my mother's body
                          so close to sleep I felt
the farm sliding in water, myself
growing crafty as a farmer, all of it
hovered   on the edge of outcry.

A first, frail paradise, where the dream
let down like tendrils, entering
through air the airless sponge
that would some time be memory. Behind the door
the pale blue Child-of-Mary cape; unfamiliar
coats; spittle, pipe smell. Drifting in
with an animal wholeness
through the propped window   the birds
(their beaks opening with the slowness of fire)
stung at the trees. Your father
held out the sovereigns to us
in their shapely box, roughened
by his hands.

And you lived thereafter
in the unlike house, whose roselight
side-windows shed ovals where the dust
shimmered always with its few motes,
and the sunlight entered from the north.
Room by room you circled it,
open as a razor; walked out
carrying the axe
into sunlight, quivered with the fowls, but
let me see
your arms froth in the entrails: fine-brown-featured
and tense, like a surviving Brontë.

Internment

They have him squeezed   into the square room
Patrick Shivers   stripped naked   a tight bag
covering his head   feet splayed   rope round his neck
all day   for fourteen hours
fingers tight against the wall   blood hammered back
into his hands   his brain screaming with a noise
as of compressed air   his mouth without water
scum filling his lips

of the right age, Catholic, the right sort,
                he will stay there
useless as a twig   his shadow
soaking into the floor underneath him

and during this time he began to think of
his son, 'The youngster
who had died at six months old'
'I prayed that God would not let me
go insane.' 'One time
I thought or imagined I had died.
Could not see youngster's face, but felt
reconciled to death. Felt happy.'

And 'during this time
no words spoken at all   bag still
over my head   I did not speak,
but prayed out loud.
Noise going all the time.'
'I tried to speak. Could only whisper
"Why did you do this to me?"
Man behind me holding bag pulled me
said, "Speak up, I can't hear you." '

Patrick Shivers
a mouthful of water after five days.

Teaching German Literature

I teach German literature, and this is how it goes:
Schiller, Böll and Hölderlin, and everybody knows
that Bertolt turned on Thomas Mann and punched him on
    the nose,
and Goethe married Clara Kronk and Clara married
    Wagner.

Hardy is a Proximist, and Philip Larkin hates
walking past the neighbours' children hanging on the gates.
Keats was orphaned, Donne was bent, and Shelley went
    out drowning,
and Wordsworth married Sara Dronk and Sara married
    Browning.

T. S. Eliot, marvellous boy, grew up with a mitre;
even in dark Russell Square you wouldn't find much
    brighter,
Fürster Rilke knew a duchess, Trudi von Bachbeiter,
and Mara married Pablo Yeats and Pablo never married.

The greats of German literature are in the dressing room,
Lotte Lenya, Suky Tawdry, fending off life's gloom,
Hans Otto Eller Manzenberger smiling at his poem,
and Clara married Leslie Liszt and Leslie married Magna.

And Goethe married Clara Kronk and Clara married
    Wagner.

Bruce Beaver (1928–   )

from *Letters to Live Poets*

I

God knows what was done to you.
I may never find out fully.
The truth reaches us slowly here,
is delayed in the mail continually
or censored in the tabloids. The war
now into its third year
remains undeclared.
The number of infants, among others, blistered
and skinned alive by napalm
has been exaggerated
by both sides we are told,
and the gas does not seriously harm;
does not kill but is merely
unbearably nauseating.
Apparently none of this
is happening to us.

I meant to write to you more than a year
ago. Then there was as much to hear,
as much to tell.
There was the black plastic monster
prefiguring hell
displayed on the roof
of the shark aquarium at the wharf.
At Surfers' Paradise were Meter Maids
glabrous in gold bikinis.
It was before your country's
president came among us like a formidable
virus. Even afterwards –
after I heard (unbelievingly)
you had been run down on an island

by a machine
apparently while renewing yourself;
that things were terminal again –
even then I might have written.

But enough of that. I could tell by the tone
of your verses there were times
when you had ranged around you,
looking for a lift from the gift horse,
your kingdom for a Pegasus.
But to be trampled by the machine
beyond protest . . .

I don't have to praise you; at least
I can say I had ears for your voice
but none of that really matters now.
Crushed though. Crushed on the littered sands.
Given the *coup de grâce* of an empty beer can,
out of sight of the 'lordly and isolate satyrs'.
Could it have happened anywhere else
than in your country, keyed to obsolescence?

I make these words perform for you
knowing though you are dead, that you 'historically
belong to the enormous bliss of American death',
that your talkative poems remain
among the living things
of the sad, embattled beach-head.

Say that I am, as ever, the young-
old fictor of communications.
It's not that I wish to avoid
talking to myself or singing
the one-sided song.
It's simply that I've come to be
more conscious of the community
world-wide, of live, mortal poets.
Moving about the circumference
I pause each day

and speak to you and you.
I haven't many answers, few
enough; fewer questions left.
Even when I'm challenged 'Who
goes there?' I give ambiguous
replies as though the self linking
heart and mind had become a gap.

You see, we have that much in common
already. It's only when I stop
thinking of you living I remember
near by our home there's an aquarium
that people pay admission to,
watching sharks at feeding time:
the white, jagged rictus in the grey
sliding anonymity,
faint blur of red through green,
the continually spreading stain.

I have to live near this, if not quite with it.
I realize there's an equivalent
in every town and city in the world.
Writing to you keeps the local, intent
shark-watchers at bay
(who if they thought at all
would think me some kind of ghoul);
rings a bell for the gilded coin-slots
at the Gold Coast;
sends the president parliament's head on a platter;
writes Vietnam like a huge four-letter
word in blood and faeces on the walls
of government; reminds me when
the intricate machine stalls
there's a poet still living at this address.

XVI

Our street is known as the street of widows.
Seven of its residents, including my mother,
have survived their husbands.
But two of the seven have weak hearts.
They listen to themselves living.

This morning at 4 a.m. a storm broke overhead.
So fierce it was, a cloudburst.
The pelting wet and cracking thunder
skinned me of sleep. I lay sickly
with a dry mouth and knotted gut,
hearing the sizzling crack of lightning's javelins.
I had a target
throbbing in my heart.
I thought of the bereaved women
and of my wife beside me
whose quiet, innate calm
would outbluff any storm.
'Grant her a winner's heart
and residual courage,' I prayed
in melodramatic silence
between thunder claps.

The huge wash of rain came through
the kitchen's roof, soaking the floor.
The electric point spat and stank
and the fire worry returned.
What would I save first,
clothes or manuscripts?
The latter would not buy me a shirt.
I saw us all barefooted in the chilly
streaming gutter under the dribbling
pine, water and fire contending
at dead of night in the morning,
time of sick dreams and lonely vigils.
But *the poet is the true stealer of fire*
I told myself, doubtingly.

Now in the dull light of the washed-out
day the old and the young women
of the street rehearse their roles
of mothers, wives, survivors.
I alone am the witnessing male
of their floured and peeled existence,
the sole drone immune to their stinging gaze.
Their sunshine squeaks and twitches
from the electric machines. The ordinary,
distorted voices of the announcers drone and bleat;
the hogwash of muzak slops
and spills about their doughy ears.

Everywhere but in this faded
street is life. Everywhere
is living. Is this street.
And the pines
drip with doves. Seagulls
spot the biscuit-coloured beach
with white. The rain-pocked sands
suck the wet down to the base of
rock. The holiday kids crouch
in shelters, eating chips, combing
hair, smelling each other's transistors,
their sex bursting from faded denim.

Thinking of them all the long, wet morning
I'm almost glad I was born middle-aged.
I process raisins from the sourest grapes
and spit the pips into the morning's maw.

XXI

Walking in late afternoon
we paused by the seawall,
saw what the storms had done,
undoing the beach by South Steyne,
breaching the wall, laving away
the sand. We stood near Queenscliff
watching the sunset sky and water,
waves light and opalescent,
sand bars near the shore, thin skin
of wet glazing blue and fawn.

Apricots, peaches and pink roses
blossoming from west to east.
Blackest of black dogs charcoaling
shadow, nosing in sand and scampering
about between the ball-throwing
last-light-halo'd father and small son.
Beside us black-habited nuns
watching waves for the water walking
red wet-suited surfer paddling
out towards night on a yellow board.
The air still prematurely full of
summer smells: heavy salt
and light, sweet fragrance of lotion.

Of all my share of sunsets,
calm tides and the balmy tug
of spring air cooling from the east,
this one was, if *nothing special*,
something still to celebrate.

Waking I walk with, sleeping lie with
you, and you make all my days
possible; to every poem
I sign our name – not one is made
without you. Should I make you known
as a woman with a warm smile,
clear eyes never averted
from the light and dark of life;
a sane mind in a sound body;
one who sings yet cannot whistle?
With you I live and am
grateful for whatever I give
and take of the day. A lyric is
in order here – but no more moralizing
in and out of verse (for today
at least). The something to say is all
in the saying. Not so much
a *negative capability* as an
estimate of potentiality.

Let me sing of our being
here and of our witnessing
the evening come to such good terms
with the sun that gold is omnipresent
as a bonus to the watchers.
Though the pines by the shore are thinned
of foliage and some of their branches are dying,
the trees aren't going to lie down
to the rhetoric of wind and rain
or the moralizing of the waves
now or in the immediate, doubtless
from time to time stormy, future.

XXXI

Soft misty rain and a drop of thirty degrees.
The need for heat again, of warm clothes.
The night is hushed in the street outside but the waves
break bleakly in a rising wash from the narrowed beach
where yesterday the crowd lolled,
reeking of oily lotion.
We walked along the shore in the early evening
baring our feet to the powdery sand
and the chill foam, the beach littered
with paper scraps and beer cans.
When we climbed the steps to the promenade
the wind tore up from the south
belabouring trees and spreading fine
sand on the bitumen of the road
hardening under the chill blast.
Sand, leaves, paper scraps and
scurrying bodies, heads covered
with huge towels, pink and brown
flanks stung by the hissing sand.
The cough and burr of cars starting,
the roar of bikes, the scratchy echo
of a thousand transistor
radios drowned in rushing wind.

We returned after the heat
to the creaking house, shrinking under
the brute back-hander of the southerly
buster. All night long the house
shrank while the weather grew into
a grey and weeping giantess of rain.
Our dreams were troubled,
all of a grey lamentation.
Waking came with a lead weight
of eyes and limbs. All day I crouched
over a book and breathed through wool
draped scarf-wise about my neck
the graphite smell of wet air.

My aching neck that changes gear
from hour to hour. For all this
I'd sooner the cool than the heat that threw me
into the mad contending ring
of blood heat and aberrant rage
against the essence of this life.
Anger's washed out again,
bleached to a tic of pale remorse.
If there's a tide recessional
within me, there's a rising tide
down there at the shore,
I hear it surge and race.
It will tear at the beach's body until
the bones of rock show through. It comes
from half-way round the world. It goes
over everything and nothingness.
Over the monsters and the mild-eyed
hippocampi. Swoosh! it comes
and Swash! it goes, and I'll stay put
until tomorrow wakes and breaks the spell.

from *Lauds and Plaints*

XIX

To C.K.

to stand hushed an hour or so
in that garden is not to redeem

time like the old man said   the old
Christian man who was almost a poet

most of the time   really a poet
some of the time   to stand looking

not really watching but being a part
of the watching   participant

[144]

amidst the trees the flowers the flowering
bushes   steeped in that colour scent

and business of growth and becoming
everywhere in the sights smells sounds

and the touch-taste of her not-quite-visible
self   an oblique glimpse in the flashing

wing of the green and crimson the cobalt
and ebony of inquisitive birds

of autumn's summery spring at winter's
wane   the perennial she   Kore

ambivalent towards blatancies
of life-surge   aware already

of the ebb of autumnal womanhood
she stands upon the verge of sight

behind a veil of willow leaf
I look past my eyes into

a shattering prism   the sight-confusing
blaze and drench of emanating

colours from an incarnating
spectrum   on every tree a mass

of leaf   on every leaf a gaudy
bug   on every bug another

gaudier yet   a glorious rout
of armorial exquisites   the spindle

legs and casque-heads   burnished breast-plates
brilliant ruby blazons   old

gold-dusted silver wings
arabesques of antennae

emerald enamelled amethystine
spilled and living treasure of the

teeming garden   leaf and blossom
honey-meading all the air

about me   I become the authentic
sempiternal drunk in springtime

no more farewells   nevermore
nostalgia   and the springtime's girl

goddess Kore Kore walking
always on the edge of things

come back to earth   come into life
and learn what you already know

the ordinary miracle of
here and now within an earthly

garden   I the older am the
younger   forever younger here

before the mistress of the magic
mundane garden   I stand and witness

earth turning towards the sun
again and winter's featureless

armour slips from me melting in the
snap and click of the insects' fiery

dialogue   the harsh sweet metrics
of their lust to be and make

the shadow of the house presides
and pointing to the east reminds me

of the westering hour   the time
has come to leave the garden   was it

always as difficult as this
the next time always is the first

Peter Porter (1929–   )

Once Bitten, Twice Bitten; Once Shy, Twice Shy

The trap setter in a steel dawn
Picks up his dead rabbits and goes home
Whistling: his tune lies over the wet fields
In the shrinking morning shadows.
The gift of morning life brings
Five broken backs for the rabbits
Dangling in his hessian wrap.
In his own house an old mother
Wastes herself for a busy cancer,
She has always sacrificed flesh and time
For others – a thin heart hates a fat man
In the same room of waiting,
And outside, two children chase
A cockerel from a hen; their sister,
In love with a school teacher,
Pushes back the sex in her measuring blouse.
Now the house basks in bridal sun
Brimming with doves. This is where
The dead rabbits come, giving life
To the fat dog and his mange and the tired wife
Dried by the recurring sun of her kitchen.
Now it is electric eleven o'clock – the stewing meat
Smells savoury past the pruned back roses
And wafts on the street's spindly limits,
The only fragrance of defence and love.

The Easiest Room in Hell

At the top of the stairs is a room
one may speak of only in parables.

It is the childhood attic,
the place to go when love has worn away,
the origin of the smell of self.

We came here on a clandestine visit
and in the full fire of indifference.

We sorted out books and let the children
sleep here away from creatures.

From its windows, ruled by willows,
the flatlands of childhood stretched
to the watermeadows.

It was the site of a massacre,
of the running down of the body
to less even than the soul,
the tribe's revenge on everything.

It was the heart of England
where the ballerinas were on points
and locums laughed through every evening.

Once it held all the games,
Inconsequences, *Misalliance*, *Frustration*,
even *Mendacity*, *Adultery* and *Manic Depression*.

But that was just its alibi,
all along it was home,
a home away from home.

Having such a sanctuary
we who parted here
will be reunited here.

You asked in an uncharacteristic note,
'Dwell I but in the suburbs
of your good pleasure?'

I replied, 'To us has been allowed
the easiest room in hell.'

Once it belonged to you,
now it is only mine.

Non Piangere, Liù

A card comes to tell you
you should report
to have your eyes tested.

But your eyes melted in the fire
and the only tears, which soon dried,
fell in the chapel.

Other things still come –
invoices, subscription renewals,
shiny plastic cards promising credit –
not much for a life spent
in the service of reality.

You need answer none of them.
Nor my asking you for one drop
of succour in my own hell.

Do not cry, I tell myself,
the whole thing is a comedy
and comedies end happily.

The fire will come out of the sun
and I shall look in the heart of it.

[150]

Good Ghost, Gaunt Ghost

She is coming towards me,
looking at me to turn me to stone,
saying my name and turning herself
into territories I know from books,
into the damned who are behind blinds.
the peaceful madmen of the parish.

She has walked through an invisible screen
into the fire of every change,
a certificate of final adaptability –
she will dress in a novel
and loiter, as is usual, in a dream,
but that is accountability.

Her clothes are syntax, so that I read
someone else's poem and I am there
on the banks of salvation
or crying in a furnace. Why has thou
held talent above my head
and let me see it, O my God?

Her shadow is rational, rationed of
tears and nocturnal commissions
saying the ego is always sublime,
the sublime always anticipatory,
and shadows our sisters under the skin:
each time we return to earth we die.

Words importing the masculine gender
include the feminine gender. Exactly,
and I see her as my hero-coward
who has dared to be myself, erasing
caution and suspicion. Soon I will be her
and we shall keep creation to ourselves.

R. A. Simpson (1929–   )

Tram Driver's Song

I stop. I go again.
The bell commands above my head.
Next stop the province of the mad.
Twelve elephants are climbing on –
A lady, sad,
Who should be dead.
Hold on. Hold on.

I go. I stop again.
The bell goes ringing down my brain.
The terminus looms up like hell.
A walrus has just slithered on –
The tram is a spell
I must sustain.
Hold on. Hold on.

I die. I'm born again.
The bell is holy and like Mass –
And look, I rise above the ground.
The people marvel, can't get on.
There was no sound.
I've turned to gas.
Hold on. Hold on.

To My Mother

My mother has lived
hoping to win a lottery.
Eighty-three
she buys her tickets,
watches TV.

I can't talk to her.
She's almost deaf but hears
what she wants to hear.
What she sees in me
is clear –

a son going his way
without much care for her,
seeing her at times,
offering money,
worried more about rhymes.

I hope she wins,
her number picked from
the barrel and read
in the auditorium
and envied by the almost dead.

Old Children

They wander near the estuary
shoeless, but proud skeletons

almost; their skin as old
as stained and sun-tanned maps –

worn-out linoleum.
They watch for broken glass

as sharp as young girls' eyes,
and pick up shells and twigs

and throw these at eternity
encroaching up the sand; their hands

too stiff to hold much now.
They see their guardian coming,

and she is dressed in white
(not black) and soon will take

them to the unlit cave
where bed is always

and no-one cries.

Bruce Dawe (1930–   )

Clouds

I am always here leaning against the fog
saying, Is that you?
                              Melbourne is like a distant war
in which I lost my life and gained some ghostly
wounds that ache when the weather's raw.

Clouds soar over the rim of the mild range,
spinning backwards blown by vast presences
who wish to remain anonymous; the whole aspect
fumes with light; we look up, we make obeisances

to the blue, the rollicking air, the sun in its bottle.
When, later, the darkened jaws of the hills
leap with the toothache of lightning and thunder cracks
its ceremonial stones together, something shrills

in us, puts on emu feathers under the Embassy shirt,
and dances. Here the poems are all
cloud-poems. To be dominated in this way,
to be drawn up thus, is deplorable!

I scratch the quick-silver at the back of old memories
until only my hand shows through. A cloud
takes shape on the page. Not again! you say, leaning over
   my shoulder.
(I avert my breath in reply, like a drunkard.)

Husband and Wife

The old jokes aren't as funny as they were,
Nor the old jokers
– Trailing in from the sun on a hot day
Almost have meaning in an unmeant way,
Disintegrates into an easy-chair, cries 'Phew!'
As if he'd nearly missed a vital cue:
'I must be getting old or something, Ann!'
Who turns and puts an arm about this man
(Incipient baldness being one more tree
Notched on the bush-track of eternity)
And rubs her face against his, saying: 'You
and me both, brother!' and the rest
Is silence (as it should be).
                        This seems best,
To mark the sweet breath of the half-mown lawn,
Not knowing whether to rejoice or mourn,
Summer trimming the hedge with shears of light,
While both of them, respectful of the night,
Kiss in the indoor dusk, even as they do
Making each sharp particular thing less true.

Drifters

One day soon he'll tell her it's time to start packing,
and the kids will yell 'Truly?' and get wildly excited for no
    reason,
and the brown kelpie pup will start dashing about, tripping
    everyone up,
and she'll go out to the vegetable-patch and pick all the
    green tomatoes from the vines,
and notice how the oldest girl is close to tears because she
    was happy here,
and how the youngest girl is beaming because she wasn't.
And the first thing she'll put on the trailer will be the
    bottling-set she never unpacked from Grovedale,

and when the loaded ute bumps down the drive past the
   blackberry-canes with their last shrivelled fruit,
she won't even ask why they're leaving this time, or where
   they're heading for
– she'll only remember how, when they came here,
she held out her hands bright with berries,
the first of the season, and said:
'Make a wish, Tom, make a wish.'

Homecoming

All day, day after day, they're bringing them home,
they're picking them up, those they can find, and bringing
   them home,
they're bringing them in, piled on the hulls of Grants, in
   trucks, in convoys,
they're zipping them up in green plastic bags,
they're tagging them now in Saigon, in the mortuary coolness
they're giving them names, they're rolling them out of
the deep-freeze lockers – on the tarmac at Tan Son Nhut
the noble jets are whining like hounds,
they are bringing them home
– curly-heads, kinky-hairs, crew-cuts, balding non-coms
– they're high, now, high and higher, over the land, the
   steaming *chow mein*,
their shadows are tracing the blue curve of the Pacific
with sorrowful quick fingers, heading south, heading east,
home, home, home – and the coasts swing upward, the old
   ridiculous curvatures
of earth, the knuckled hills, the mangrove-swamps, the
   desert emptiness . . .
in their sterile housing they tilt towards these like skiers
– taxiing in, on the long runways, the howl of their
   homecoming rises
surrounding them like their last moments (the mash, the
   splendour)
then fading at length as they move

on to small towns where dogs in the frozen sunset
raise muzzles in mute salute,
and on to cities in whose wide web of suburbs
telegrams tremble like leaves from a wintering tree
and the spider grief swings in his bitter geometry
– they're bringing them home, now, too late, too early.

Weapons Training

And when I say eyes right I want to hear
those eyeballs click and the gentle pitter-patter
of falling dandruff   you there what's the matter
why are you looking at me   are you a queer?
look to your front   if you had one more brain
it'd be lonely   what are you laughing at
you in the back row with the unsightly fat
between your elephant ears   open that drain
you call a mind and listen   remember first
the cockpit drill when you go down   be sure
the old crown-jewels are safely tucked away   what could be
   more
distressing than to hold off with a burst
from your trusty weapon a mob of the little yellows
only to find back home because of your position
your chances of turning the key in the ignition
considerably reduced?   allright now suppose
for the sake of argument you've got
a number-one blockage and a brand-new pack
of Charlies are coming at you   you can smell their rotten
                                   fish-sauce breath hot on the back
of your stupid neck allright now what
are you going to do about it?   that's right grab and check
the magazine man it's not a woman's tit
worse luck or you'd be set   too late you nit
they're on you and your tripes are round your neck
you've copped the bloody lot just like I said
and you know what you are?   you're dead dead dead

The Christ of the Abyss

In the waters off Portofino
the Christ of the Abyss
holds wide His arms
to the coral-divers drowning with their last baskets of red
    coral around their necks,
to the spear-fishermen's fish, the amber-jack twisting on the
    bright barb,
to the tourists' polaroid lenses spinning down through the
    lime waves like thrown coins
– like the Christ of the Upper Air, the Christ of the Andes,
He draws all men unto Him, the little souls
circling in like fish
with their cries and concerns
mute gleams in the wanlight . . .

And the waters go over Him like air,
and like the fragile ancient amphora
bringing wine and grain to the great sea's shores
He outlasts both timber and iron, trireme and motor-cruiser,
the salt,
            and the weed,
                        and the slime.

Philip Martin (1931–)

Nursing Home

Incontinence, and the mind going. Where?
The place is all it should be. Not enough.
She's had such spirit. *No more advice, thank you!*
And she'd slam down the receiver. Hated drudging:
The house is crawling away with dirt, but I'm
Going out to garden. Thwarted, self-thwarted:
Gave up the piano when her marriage failed,
Should have had a career. Instead she moved:
Twenty houses in forty years. And always
Well, dear son, at last we've found the right one.
Never. And now, this one room, to be shared
With a woman still as a stonefish.
                                        Sunday morning:
Outside, the trees wrestle with spring wind.
She sits here in her chair beating her tray:
Sister sister sister sister sister!
Clenches her lips, hums against them. And again
Sister sister sister sister sister!
High, scratched voice: *Behind me behind me behind me!*
What is, Mother? A pause. *I don't know.*
And again the drumming: *Sister sister sister!*

The mind going, and coming back, and going.
Each ebb, a little further. She says one evening
A bit flat today. Long pause, and then
I don't like this place. (What is *this place*?)
And slowly: *All that way along that wall!*
Too far to go.

I stand smoothing her forehead,
Her child's become her parent, saying with her
The night prayers. She's growing peaceful now.
I'm drawn to the edge of a mystery. The mind
I cannot know, what does it know? She seems
Listening. As a remote landscape listens
To its river in a circle of hills. As a boat
Far out may heed the current beneath,
Bearing it further. What sounds? To us, silence.

Evan Jones (1931–   )

The Falling Sickness

The foliage of light begins to wither
Into a dark discontinuity,
And in that darkness now I bring together
A pattern of disorder, tenuously:

Dim squares of light and shade, this music and these voices.
Under the skin and flesh my fingers feel
The fine erratic structure that encases
The focus of all movement. I lie still.

Now in a little while this world that I
Could shut out with a hand will take its sway
Till I have misremembered that outcry
And stagger forward into yesterday.

Hostel

Eyes on the plate – the scoop of mashed potato,
The black roast lamb – but slyly look around:
This was a queer place now to go to ground
You poor old fox, your head crammed full of Plato
And stuff like that. Now careful, not a sound.

Somebody nods: just nod, don't risk a smile.
Ten minutes flat should see us out again:
Then you can go and lie down in your den
Behind a locked door. But snap this for the file:
Men: men of all shapes and sizes: single men.

On Sundays everybody stays at home
Shut in his room, except that someone plays
The old piano. Lying in a daze
I wonder how so many sounds can come
Even through these walls. I can't miss a phrase.

At night I hear the light switch off next door,
The bed creak and the cough and the nose blown,
Feet up and down the corridor, the drone
Of distant voices: and I settle down.
That's why we like it, that's what we're here for:
Nobody feels at night that he's alone.

A Line from Keats

The south-coast sun, the play of light and air,
The rain, indeed, and all that various weather,
Mirrored all our delight and wantonness.
Breath could move your ruffled hair
As we lay there at last at peace together,
Perfect and unconcerned in nakedness.

Moments of discord swelled up and were gone:
I stalked out once into the feathery rain
And drove away, because you would not call me.
I came back with my tarnished honours on
Within an hour; at once you made it plain
That you would spare no effort to enthral me.

It was my darling here, my darling there
As we joined in a clear festivity
Needing no celebration,
Needing no more occasion than our bare
Desire to come together: you and I,
Bright in that burning week of consummation.

All stories, you once said, should have this end:
To change the burden slightly, *long ago*
These lovers fled away into the calm.
Easily I became your 'dearest friend'
And now am someone that you scarcely know,
A memory that you balance in your palm.

Honeymoon, South Coast

Sometime shortly after the rain began
    A quarrel began also:
Fish, chess, magazines and toothpaste
    Fed into an argument that ran,
        Alto and basso,
        Through stave on stave of waste.

All night the water shambled on sand,
    The wind complained poorly:
Insomniac, snoring, they lay back to back;
    Next morning they walked hand in hand,
        But insecurely,
        Through mile on mile of wrack.

Molly-hawks, ocean gulls, mostly silver gulls
    Welcomed the brighter weather
That lay along a hundred miles of coastline:
    But in the shadow of the hills
        They set out together
        Through years and years of rain.

A Solicitors' World

for Linton Lethlean

A world of lunches, conferences behind
   locked doors, negotiations
balanced on wheedling, common sense, sometimes
   something like threat, and running
on money, which after all it burns up
   faster than anything else,
when it turns its face to the light it blinks
   and hoots, owl-like, about Justice.

Who knows more about justice than this does?
   A thousand years have fed it
conundrums to codify, precedents
   for every human failing:
no wonder therefore, alas, that it should
   grunt, gurgle, and grind most things
down to a sorry slurry: from the law
   only lawyers do well. Well,

not quite: though broad enough a target for
   satire's blindest archer, this
also is a shield beneath which huddle
   misery's people, many
against all odds offered understanding,
   lenity, not always fleeced.
Not a world I wish to be embroiled in,
   yours is a world that yields men

I would sooner talk to than most.

Jennifer Strauss (1933–   )

After a Death

Last night I dreamt of the Pittsburgh tunnels
Piping the traffic under the winter hills:

To grope half-sighted in a narrow passage
Shut by the grinding weight
Of earth's bones and flesh, the thud of its rivers,
In an underground of exhausted air
Walled by a dark and pestilential pallor
Lit spasmodically by sickly glares,
The big trucks swimming up like lanterned leviathans,
Great gouts of mud and snow packed to ice
Slopped from their warmed metal underbellies.
Everything slithery – sweat along the hairline,
At the upper lip, fingers wet on the wheel,
Eyes popping at lids
Screaming for light at the end of the tunnel
Let, let, let me
(Panic of dying, panic of birth)
Out.

That's how it was in sixty-seven: a hard season.
Strange to all comers, we grew foreign
Even to each other; had to learn
A new language, to put out tentacles of trust,
To touch, grasp. Patience.
Wait for the spring, you said. At winter's end
We started our third child.
Last night I dreamt of the Pittsburgh tunnels.
I was re-making history, entering joyfully, singing,
Certain you waited in light at the tunnel's end
And I Eurydice coming to fetch you home,
Not dreaming in dreams you ever could turn away
Unteachably into the dark.

I woke too soon.
The spring wind rattling the door
Was herald to no-one but itself.
Our cycle's done: you will not come again.

Stone, Scissors, Paper

Why is the face of the dead so absolute
Like stone
It stuns the edge of grief.

Blundering in the kitchen, my knife slips,
Blood spurts from a finger, recalls
The story
Heard from one of those surgical ward survivors
How, once and far away,
Falling, he gashed a leg on his father's fishing knife
So violently he almost bled to death.

Doctored, he lay for weeks in a strange town;
His mother in their village
Gathered one day
Knives, razors, shears,
Every cutting implement in the house
To carry them up to the cliff's steepest edge
And hurl them into the sea.

In dancing fall they glitter through my mind
And Mediterranean wind
Distresses
Blackness of skirt and shawl,
But she, at the heart of the dance presiding,
Is fixed in achieved gesture
Splendid, intemperate.

This is another country, we manage differently:
Tidy our agonies to the back of shelves,
Lock up flamboyance,
And take the children driving in the car.
Subdued to unnatural goodness
(Not to disturb now) they play a gesture game:
'Stone, Scissors, Paper'.

'Stone blunts Scissors' – but bruises flesh
And the bruise spreads inwardly
Aches.
To catch at comfort, I try words:
'Paper wraps Stone' – but stone being wrapped
Unguarded
'Scissors cut Paper'.

Paper tears – but does not weep.
Beyond the terms of the game another element:
The sea that swallows up knives,
Water that wears away stone.

Fay Zwicky (1933–)

To a Sea-Horse

The male has a pouch on the underside of the tail into which the female
injects the eggs. When the eggs hatch it looks as if the male is giving birth
to the young. Even after hatching, the young remain near the father,
darting back into his pouch if danger threatens.

Wall-eyed snouter, sweet feeble translucent
Tiny eunuch teetering on your rocker,
Pouting, corseted in
Rings of bone, flesh flaps
Fanning the tides as you totter and roll
Forward, but never so forward as
She.
Flex your pipes for the winter.
Keep an upright house.
Pucker piped lips for her, flex,
Flex your rings, flash your fin
If you can, man. Watch it!
Your love's bearing down with
Transparent efficiency, that
Abrasive lady's been starching her
Dorsal for meeting, nudges
Neatly your ring-tailed poise;
Totter and flex, finny vibrato for
Sex (can't afford to go off your
Rocker at this stage),
FLEX!
Chess knights collide:
A shuddering pouchful of eggs.
Nuzzle your snouters, sweet
Sons and daughters, tip to
Your tiny transparencies,
Hatched in your warmth,
Flexed in your strength.
They'd be mad to trust women
After this.

Dreams

Sleeping badly, he'd wake in a rage
to recover the loss. Loss of what?
He could never be sure. At his age
(hardly love but a spasm perhaps?)

A tight squeeze of the heart – nothing more
he'd assure himself, breathing alone in the
darkness. Yet why did he look to the door
as if something had come and was gone?

Mysterious injury, ill and yet never quite
ill enough, it would seem (for a time)
as if she'd never been. By the light
of a day he'd see a girl walking away

In the rain – a casual profile, the turn
of a wrist, the drop of a head. She
didn't exist, had never. He'd learn
to forget, to begin to forget

He would sleep again. Obscurely and peacefully dead
to the world, breathing easy. Yet suddenly dreaming,
awake to himself in the dark of the bed, somewhere
in an endless passage started to howl.

Bat

Born bat-blind
wawled naked
into flight,
parent-pocketed
                    I swerve
from light, see through
my crazy stiffening ears.

Hang-glider of your flood
Sir, I skim
            and
                  whirl
                      dark water.

                    Struts extended,
prop thin skin against your
withering blast.

Whirring within the ark,
claws lurch to clutch at
crevice memories, the hollows
of a feeding dusk.

Come night, and Noah ducks my
fine fur, accurate flap, my
craven pointed face.

My nostrils trail spirals of
shrill screams.

I'm more afraid
did they but know what you
have always known:

by day I hang
like one condemned
to die

Chris Wallace-Crabbe (1934–   )

Losses and Recoveries

1.

There he goes, went, catch him,
small boy with a beret, nervously smiling, taken
for tourist walks on the wrong end of the leash
in that snow-white stretch of life I can't remember:
half-timbered Munich, strudelplatz Berlin,
droppings of history mounded above me,
over those pigeons the Leica had me feed.
Where's it all gone, that Deutschland culture-fodder
that I soaked up in travel, a willing sponge?

Crusty surfaces in halftone,
brick, stone, snow, inked crosses marking
a bit of my self on this or that hotel
and here's the window where I heard the Rhineland
cobbles re-echo to military geese,
but I can't know whatever I could tell,
what strands were plaited by which war, which peace.

2.

A drive flashes from the thick meat of my bat,
leaving extra cover for dead. All around us,
touched by a pastoral brush,
midges hover and glint:
chiaroscuro daubs the river-gums.
The serene hour brims with oceanic feeling,
drowning these four green ovals deep as dream
in which I move at ease, for Morrison's off-spinners
aren't going to turn an inch this afternoon.

Goings and dwindlings: my stupid adolescence,
bone-dry years of hollowness and blank,
thirsting, fills out again with fields and games
till my lifelong model
of happiness or poise becomes
a well-timed leg glance taken off my toes.

3.

for Bruce Dawe

Film has no tenses, the latest pundit says,
poems have tenses and nostalgias though
like anything, and when I get to think
of the mid-fifties, flashing through my slides,
I see you slope past Chemistry, blue-chinned
in military shirt and a maroon
figured art-silk tie with – look – I'm right –
Ciardi's *Inferno* splitting away to cantos
and well-thumbed pages in your jacket pocket,
verse on your tongue of mice in evening dress.

In memory's yellow eye it's always summer,
nobody ever worked, the grass grew thick,
coffee cups, unlike women, had no bottoms
and there you grin, old-fashioned Carlton shepherd
dry-wittedly enjoying
the Arcadian lull between Joey Cassidy stories.

4.

Looms up the liner's rivety white side,
streamers droop overhead,
our good friends go. There are many folk we love
this way and that, struggling to find a balance
where the high side fills with a charge of shadows
and wharfside waters lap quietly below.
Dulled along splintery boards we walk away.

[173]

Melbourne holds us: hands, lips, bodies, all
that we are it feeds – and feeds upon;
many would go, but drag the city with them
world-wide, wherever they push and flee.
Here, look now, all this is ourselves and
up over the dull blue skyline dangles
a bright eastering T-jet the colour of hope.

The Aftermath: Yorkshire 1644

Then there was cool dispersion everywhere,
fatigue suddenly of muscle and shoulder,
dead weight of everything our Lord had made,
face bone-dry, drawn like the skin of a drum,
all the moorland strangely quiet.
Nobody shouted.
                        My saddle creaked a rhythm,
the big piebald wearily rocked beneath me
plodding to camp along a spongy slope
terraced with sheep tracks
and while I bent my thoughts to praising God
I found some pleasure in the sharpened chill,
glorious banners of western sky,
shepherd's delight marked with a first few stars,
dark outline of trees
and the short miles left me. Giving thanks
was one thing I forgot and so forgot the killing,
being again a farmer on his horse
pressing at leisure through a clear bright evening
past the lights of scattered garths.

Childhood

Creases of the shouldery mountain
are smelling of forest,
of bark, crushed leaves
and hoarded damp
lingering on into
January's broad glare.

In the thin, creamy-brown,
cracked grass of a paddock
waiter and parlourmaid lie
in one another's sweaty arms,
her skirt rucked up
hard against his belly

while, just out of their eyes' corners,
unheeding, half-heeding Maneli
jolts around jaunty
on the hairy backbone
of a Clydesdale
at the very core of summer.

The beast's thick ventricles fill up with blood
as he bumbles on cloddy earth
with a small girl on board
and a wagtail somersaulting
thisway-thatway
all around her head.

New Carpentry

'Check it in here,' he said
squinting against the dayshine.
'Mortise and tenon. Yeah.
Chuck us over the hammer
where it's lying beside you.'
Whacking his chisel into soft splintery wood.

No metaphor
the real thing.

Cutting a piece of oregon to length,
blond sawdust flying out in puffs,
tarring the end
two inches of blackness for mother earth.

Now he drives plugs into
the old brickwork corner –
soft, friable, orange bricks –
and nails the upright into place
with a chiselled gap for lintel
four by two.

We are ready to hang the door.

Death, 1976

In these few wire-taut weeks
mother has been made over
to aspengrey ash,
her thin jaw grim to the last,
fear consorting with will,
knowing bloody well in her bed
her cancellation coming.

My first clear model of the world
was Mendeleev's periodic chart;
within its rigid scaffolding were furled
all fleeting colours that had teased the heart.
Flame-tints, metallic sheens, affinities
found their first causes ranged upon this grid
without a hint of strange interstices
or phantoms making their bid.

    Body nothing, soul gone nowhere
    other than ripplewise rolling
    among survivors. What is man
    that he should bear to breathe
    this air in this world of
    less than even air seems?
    Matter troubles us all.

Soft Eden always suffers a decline.
My long-due ticket for expulsion came
as into that design
the variegated meson thrust a name,
thrust its gold apple in five baffling forms,
destroyed all concord where I set my feet
and now I strode into electric storms
groping for light, for oxygen, for heat.

    Burn, frail person, burn.
    Substance abrades, has gone
    into ground, or figures, or flowers.
    Under a mental veil
    all vanishes. We live
    where uncertainty prevails
    as principle, as pain,

    as our invisible key.

Panoptics

It was another race
with a slender hold indeed
on the lintel of prehistory:
a graminivorous people,
gentle, bandy, greeneyed,
who left so little mark
on the tofts and crofts of time,
their adzes unremarkable,
shards pitifully few
and their passions blown away
like the long lavender wind.

They gave myth to the stars,
looked into that unbelievably
complex mosaic of
diamantine fires and
called the clusters by names:
there were The Kiss, The Groin,
The Phallus and The First Dream,
Climax and Dayspring,
The Hip, The Labia,
The Great Exploring Tongue
and Semen of the Gods.

It was another race,
gentle as rosewater,
libidinous like kittens,
who coined such poetry,
who got dusted away by process
to leave not even
their names on the starry chart
or in the sharp sand.
A new taxonomy
keeps all the stars in place
leaving our dreams alone
and the gone magicians.

Jasmine

A presence – how can you name a smell? –
heavy, hazed, like peaches and honey perhaps,
spreading over the lawns and lanes;

look to the flowers, dense on their dark-green
pointed leaves and upcurving tendrils.
They are fivefold stars of white,

they have crooked points, they are
spokes of a series of wheels turning clockwise,
there is a touch of yellow inside the corolla.

Sweetness of jasmine,
it bends up from the rickety paling fence
by untended beans and caulies.

Can such floods
of scent
come from those frail starfish

bunched high on the tennis-court wire?
The gravel swoons,
the lobs drop back.

David Malouf (1934–   )

The Year of the Foxes

for Don Anderson

When I was ten my mother, having sold
her old fox-fur (a ginger red bone-jawed
Magda Lupescu
of a fox that on her arm played
dead, cunningly dangled
a lean and tufted paw)

decided there was money to be made
from foxes, and bought via
the columns of the *Courier Mail* a whole
pack of them; they hung from penny hooks
in our panelled sitting-room, trailed from the backs
of chairs; and Brisbane ladies, rather
the worse for war, drove up in taxis wearing
a G.I. on their arm
and rang at our front door.

I slept across the hall, at night hearing
their thin cold cry. I dreamed the dangerous spark
of their eyes, brushes aflame
in our fur-hung, nomadic
tent in the suburbs, the dark fox-stink of them
cornered in their holes
and turning.   Among my mother's show pieces –
Noritaki teacups, tall hock glasses
with stems like barley-sugar,
goldleaf *demitasses* –
the foxes, row upon row, thin-nosed, prick-eared,
dead.

The cry of hounds
was lost behind mirror glass,
where ladies with silken snoods and finger-nails
of chinese lacquer red
fastened a limp paw;
went down in their high heels
to the warm soft bitumen, wearing at throat
and elbow the rare spoils
of '44; old foxes, rusty red like dried-up wounds,
and a G.I. escort.

Reading Horace outside Sydney: 1970

The distance is deceptive. Sydney glitters invisible
in its holocaust of air just thirty miles away. In Rome,
two thousand years from here, a goosequill scrapes, two
    crack divisions
are hurled against a furclad barbarous northern people
    pushing

south into history, small throats are cut at committee-tables,
a marriage dies in bed; bald officials like old pennies
worn smooth by time and trade were once my copper-keen
    school-fellows
who studied Cicero and shook their heads over the fall

of virtue in high places – now on pills, twelve storeys high
in air, they shake their heads and fall and rise and walk
    again.
Somewhere across a border shabby barefoot warriors
stumble into grass, an empire mourns, in small wars
    seeking

boundaries against death. Over the traffic, over the harbour, lions
roar, schoolboys scramble out of nightmares, mineral stocks
fall with a noiseless crash, the sigh of millions. Cicadas
are heard, shrill under stones, in the long suspension of our
  breath.

Out here wheat breathes and surges, poplars flare. On the
  highway, lorries
throb toward city squares. Off in the blue a Cessna bi-plane,
crop-dusting lucerne, turns to catch the sun. The brilliant
  granule
climbs on out of sight. Its shadow dances in my palm.

Off the Map

All night headlamps dazzle
the leaves. Truck drivers
throbbing on pills
climb out of the sleep

of farm towns prim
behind moonlit lace, bronze Anzacs
nodding, leaden-headed,
at ease between wars,

and out into a dream
of apple-orchards, paddocks
tumbling with mice,
bridges that slog the air

– black piers, bright water – silos
moonstruck, pointing nowhere,
like saints practising stillness
in the ripple of grain.

They thunder across country
like the daredevil boys
of the 'Fifties who flourished
a pistol in banks,

and rode off into headlines
and hills or into legends
that hang grey-ghostly over
campfires in the rain.

Now kids, bare-footed, wade
in the warm hatched tyre-marks
of country dust, the print
of monsters; cattle stare.

All night through the upland
spaces of our skull
in low gear shifting skyward
they climb towards dawn.

A lit butt glows, a beercan
clatters. Strung out
on the hills, new streets that shine
in the eyes of farmboys, cities

alive only at nightfall
that span a continent.
Nameless. Not to be found
by day on any map.

Randolph Stow (1935–   )

Dust

'Enough,' she said. But the dust still rained about her;
over her living-room (hideous, autumnal)
dropping its small defiance.
                              The clock turned green.
She spurned her broom and took a train. The neighbours
have heard nothing.

Jungles, deserts, stars – the six days of creation –
came floating in, gold on a chute of light.
In May, grudging farmers admired the carpet
and foretold a rich year.

Miraculous August! What shelves of yellow capeweed,
what pouffes of everlastings. We worship nature
in my country.

Never such heath as flowered on the virgin slopes
of the terrible armchairs. Never convolvulus
brighter than that which choked the china dogs.
Bushwalkers' Clubs boiled their billies with humility
in chimneys where orchids and treesnakes
luxuriantly intertwined.

A photographer came from *The West Australian*, and ten
teenage reportresses. Teachers of botany
overflowed to the garden.

Indeed, trains were run from Yalgoo and Oodnadatta.
But the neighbours slept behind sealed doors, with feather
dusters beside their beds.

Ruins of the City of Hay

The wind has scattered my city to the sheep.
Capeweed and lovely lupins choke the street
where the wind wanders in great gaunt chimneys of hay
and straws cry out like keyholes.

Our yellow Petra of the fields: alas!
I walk the ruins of forum and capitol,
through quiet squares, by the temples of tranquillity.
Wisps of the metropolis brush my hair.
I become invisible in tears.

This was no ratbags' Eden: these were true haystacks.
Golden, but functional, our mansions sprang from dreams
of architects in love (*O my meadow queen!*).
No need for fires to be lit on the yellow hearthstones;
our walls were warmer than flesh, more sure than igloos.
On winter nights we squatted naked as Esquimaux,
chanting our sagas of innocent chauvinism.

In the street no vehicle passed. No telephone,
doorbell or till was heard in the canyons of hay.
No stir, no sound, but the sickle and the loom,
and the comments of emus begging by kitchen doors
in the moonlike silence of morning.

Though the neighbour states (said Lao Tse) lie in sight of
    the city
and their cocks wake and their watchdogs warn the
    inhabitants
the men of the city of hay will never go there
all the days of their lives.

But the wind of the world descended on lovely Petra
and the spires of the towers and the statues and belfries fell.
The bones of my brothers broke in the breaking columns.
The bones of my sisters, clasping their broken children,
cracked on the hearthstones, under the rooftrees of hay.
I alone mourn in the temples, by broken altars
bowered in black nightshade and mauve salvation-jane.

And the cocks of the neighbour nations scratch in the straw.
And their dogs rejoice in the bones of all my brethren.

The Dying Chair

Vadoga, my middle-aged brother,
half a ton of tobacco
could not repay your good will
to your Dimdim friend.
When my deck chair ripped, how promptly
you shinned a palm to help me,
how skilfully you fixed it
with plaited fronds.
In that dying, elastic chair
deep, deep I foundered,
calling blessings on your name
as my spine touched ground.

Palms tell the time of day:
the softest green is morning;
at noon, a touch of copper;
at twilight, lead.
But when the mauve light faded
and Tilley lamps were lit,
and smoke crept from the eaves
of the palm-leaf houses,
my fragrant and dying chair
said my youth was passing,
and the green blood turning brown
in my stagnant veins.

Sleep

Sleep: you are my homestead, and my garden;
my self's stockade; identity's last fortress . . .

All day I have stood the siege, and my hands are shaking;
my paddocks are charred and fuming, my flocks are
    slaughtered;

my lands mirror the moon in desolation.
But the moon has come. And the tribes, like smoke, seep
    campward.

And turning, barring the wall-slits with jarrah shutters,
my rifles leaned to the door, I cede; conjuring

Sleep: who are silence; make me a hollow stone
– filled with white blowing ash, and wind, and darkness.

Starshine, or hostile beacon: all light is welded.
So far, so sweet, I know I shall some day love them,

the warchants of cicadas trill in my caverns,
and all is fused, dimmed, healed, in a general grieving.

And man I mourn; till the hurts are as wrongs in childhood
– and a child forgets; though he weep, asleep, forever . . .

Sleep: you are the month that will raise my pastures.
You are my firebreak. My homestead has not fallen.

Jimmy Woodsers

Remembering. Pools. Remembering. Eyes. Remembering
(my eyes in the mirror, my eyes among the bottles)
my eyes: dry pools, in the waterless country.

The pool is empty now beneath the olives,
drained for the safety of the little cousins,
who are now tall men, and safe, in the waterless country.

My grandmother's long white hair wept in the basin.
Gumtrees stooped and crippled by the southerly
were ladies washing their long green hair, remembering.

Green: the green explosions of May, the August fires.
Rampaging radish ambushed a sleeping train
and held it, for a season, hooting through flowers,
wreathed, leaved, unheard, remembering.

The olives drizzled; green petals, abortive fruit
on the undrained pool. Then, like a storm, November,
and among the sunflowers, behind the oleander,
gulls assembled to mock my calamitous birth.

The bitter wind bent all my trees to northward.
The sea at each end of the street advanced to meet me.
On a morning in March I said goodday to time,
and doves and all went down in the blowing dunes.

In the white smoke of the sand remembering
today and the grey smoke of my lips on the glass
I set out again for the clay-pans of my eyes,

crying: 'My friend. You must drove your sheep elsewhere.
My dams are dry. You must leave this waterless country.'

Thomas Shapcott (1935–)

The Litanies of Julia Pastrana (1832–1860)

I

The Lord's name be praised
  for the health that keeps me performing my tasks each
  day without faltering.
The Lord's name be praised
  for my very tidy figure and the good strength
  of my spine
  to keep me agile in dancing.
The Lord's name be hallowed
  for the sharpness of my eyes and the excellent
  juices of my digestion.
I am in debt to the Lord
  for all things even my present employment –
  I who could
  have withered on
  the dustheap of the high village am enabled to travel to
  the curious and
  enquiring Capitals of Europe –
I am in debt to the Lord for all things
  even my present expectations
  for my Manager has made me a proposal of marriage. He
  loves me for my own sake.
I am indebted to the Lord of all things.
  My body covered with hair that made me cringe in the
  dark from the
  village stone throwers has earned me true fortune and
  undreamt of advantages,
  my double row of teeth set in this bearded thick jaw that
  frightened even
  myself as a child looking in the well with its cruel
  reflections the Lord has
  made for me to be a wonder to the learned physicians
  of London,

my wide thick nostrils that they called me ape-baby for
in those terrible
village days are no more strange in the Lord's eye
than the immensely
varied noses I see in the gaping audiences who are
compelled to suffer
without any rewards,
The Lord's name be hallowed and praised
    for I have been instructed to consider all my born
    qualities as accomplishments.

In my own tongue I sing a soft theme to the Lord,
In my own heart I dance with quietness –
    not so loud that the sightseers will hear me;
    yet when I have a
new dress I remember its price and its prettiness,
I hold myself
straight and proud – the Lord knows there is
beauty in the long
black hair that covers my body. Let them see,
let them stare. The
Lord knows that. He gives me pride in that. They pay
their pennies
and I dance snappingly for their pennies and for
the money my Manager
is keeping for me and for the Praise: the praise I say, of
the good Lord
the brother of understanding
who was himself many days in the desert and was jeered
at and has my
heart in his dear keeping.

    II

Why do I dream in my lungs
high air and mountain tightness?
I will never return there.
I had brothers led the chase and the hunt
has me still panting, awake with strained

unweeping eyes from my mattress of goosefeathers.
I had a father.
How the heart winces across years
how the smallest flower is remembered
the first blows.
The Lord trembled for me in those years.
High air of Mexico, still claimant over me.

These European sea coast cities burden themselves
sometimes it is like a feeling of
being within intestines,
sometimes it is like
cells, not an open cage.
But to move constantly
(I move protected by blinds and veils)
is the Lord's way, who travelled
and was also homeless.

III

'The Ugliest Woman in the World'
dances for your patronage
and your curiosity,
you curious ones
you with pink faces and puffy eyes and hands stuffed
   into tight cloth purchased with broken mountains
you with sour mouths hiding bone-yellow
   teeth that have chewed
   upon the produce of a quarry of blind children
you with delicate complexions powdered from the estates
   of pork barons and blood-slimy dealers in villages
you festering citizens of the bulbous pendulous cities
   you breathers of discharged curses, brothers of God
   yea even brothers

IV

My red tinsel dress – will he tear roubles and banknotes
   into the Volga

managing my dowry – I told him I would adore I had
   such spirits in me he
was abashed then delighted he implored again – I tell you he
   implored, God,
and I had you, praise you, for the good things in my body
   – how he liked
me trim in red tinsel how he – is it now – my child will be
   – like you,
Lord, will be tall and fair and with a good strong spine to
   walk upright –
and without shadows and veils – is it always like this,
   the pain is
enlarging too widely – he will be with shiny black hair and
   black eyes they
can be my gift to him and the dance and strut of a proud man
   – God the way
my father had a strut in the plaza – it is coming yet? how
   many hours do you
have cloth to mop me, all the hair on my body drags as never
   before, all my
body over the matted hair is heavy down, sodden – it is to
   be, Lord, OPENING

V

THE MUMMIFIED APE WOMAN AND THE MUMMY
   CHILD glassed,
strung on a perch like a parrot, the child. How grotesque!
Look closer:
how terribly real, not like a waxwork at all but almost human.
Lord!
Give thanks never to have
seen them
real
and alive
among
us.

Les A. Murray (1938–)

Driving through Sawmill Towns

1.

In the high cool country,
having come from the clouds,
down a tilting road
into a distant valley,
you drive without haste. Your windscreen parts the forest,
swaying and glancing, and jammed midday brilliance
crouches in clearings . . .
then you come across them,
the sawmill towns, bare hamlets built of boards
with perhaps a store,
perhaps a bridge beyond
and a little sidelong creek alive with pebbles.

2.

The mills are roofed with iron, have no walls:
you look straight in as you pass, see lithe men working,
the swerve of a winch,
dim dazzling blades advancing
through a trolley-borne trunk
till it sags apart
in a manifold sprawl of weatherboards and battens.

The men watch you pass:
when you stop your car and ask them for directions,
tall youths look away –
it is the older men who
come out in blue singlets and talk softly to you.

Beside each mill, smoke trickles out of mounds
of ash and sawdust.

3.

You glide on through town,
your mudguards damp with cloud.
The houses there wear verandahs out of shyness,
all day in calendared kitchens, women listen
for cars on the road,
lost children in the bush,
a cry from the mill, a footstep –
nothing happens.

The half-heard radio sings
its song of sidewalks.

Sometimes a woman, sweeping her front step,
or a plain young wife at a tankstand fetching water
in a metal bucket will turn round and gaze
at the mountains in wonderment,
looking for a city.

4.

Evenings are very quiet. All around
the forest is there.
As night comes down, the houses watch each other:
a light going out in a window here has meaning.

You speed away through the upland,
glare through towns
and are gone in the forest, glowing on far hills.

On summer nights
ground-crickets sing and pause.
In the dark of winter, tin roofs sough with rain,
downpipes chafe in the wind, agog with water.
Men sit after tea
by the stove while their wives talk, rolling a dead match
between their fingers,
thinking of the future.

from *Evening Alone at Bunyah*

III

There is a glow in the kitchen window now
that was not there in the old days. They have set
three streetlights up along the Gloucester road
for cows to stray by, and night birds to shun,
for the road itself's not paved, and there's no town
in the valley yet at all.
It is hoped there will be.

Today, out walking, I considered stones.
It used to be said that I must know each one
on the road by its first name, I was such a dawdler,
such a head-down starer.
I picked up
a chunk of milk-seamed quartz, thumbed off the clay,
let the dry light pervade it and collect,
eliciting shifting gleams, revealing how
the specific strength of a stone fits utterly
into its form and yet reflects the grain
and tendency of the mother-lode, the mass
of a vanished rock-sill tipping one small stone
slightly askew as it weighs upon your palm,
and then I threw it back towards the sun
to thump down on a knoll
where it may move a foot in a thousand years.

Today, having come back, summer was all mirror
tormenting me. I fled down cattle tracks
chest-deep in the earth, and pushed in under twigs
to sit by cool water seeping over rims
of blackened basalt, the tall light reaching me.

Since those moth-grimed streetlamps came,
my dark is threatened.

An Absolutely Ordinary Rainbow

The word goes round Repins,
the murmur goes round Lorenzinis,
at Tattersalls, men look up from sheets of numbers,
the Stock Exchange scribblers forget the chalk in their hands
and men with bread in their pockets leave the Greek Club:
There's a fellow crying in Martin Place. They can't stop him.

The traffic in George Street is banked up for half a mile
and drained of motion. The crowds are edgy with talk
and more crowds come hurrying. Many run in the back
    streets
which minutes ago were busy main streets, pointing:
There's a fellow weeping down there. No one can stop him.

The man we surround, the man no one approaches
simply weeps, and does not cover it, weeps
not like a child, not like the wind, like a man
and does not declaim it, nor beat his breast, nor even
sob very loudly – yet the dignity of his weeping

holds us back from his space, the hollow he makes about
    him
in the midday light, in his pentagram of sorrow,
and uniforms back in the crowd who tried to seize him
stare out at him, and feel, with amazement, their minds
longing for tears as children for a rainbow.

Some will say, in the years to come, a halo
or force stood around him. There is no such thing.
Some will say they were shocked and would have stopped
    him
but they will not have been there. The fiercest manhood,
the toughest reserve, the slickest wit amongst us

trembles with silence, and burns with unexpected
judgements of peace. Some in the concourse scream
who thought themselves happy. Only the smallest children
and such as look out of Paradise come near him
and sit at his feet, with dogs and dusty pigeons.

Ridiculous, says a man near me, and stops
his mouth with his hands, as if it uttered vomit –
and I see a woman, shining, stretch her hand
and shake as she receives the gift of weeping;
as many as follow her also receive it

and many weep for sheer acceptance, and more
refuse to weep for fear of all acceptance,
but the weeping man, like the earth, requires nothing,
the man who weeps ignores us, and cries out
of his writhen face and ordinary body

not words, but grief, not messages, but sorrow
hard as the earth, sheer, present as the sea –
and when he stops, he simply walks between us
mopping his face with the dignity of one
man who has wept, and now has finished weeping.

Evading believers, he hurries off down Pitt Street.

from *Walking to the Cattle Place*

2.

Birds in Their Title Work Freeholds of Straw

At the hour I slept
kitchen lamps were sending out barefoot children
muzzy with stars and milk thistles
stoning up cows.
They will never forget their quick-fade cow-piss slippers
nor chasing such warmth over white frost, saffron to steam.
It will make them sad bankers.

[197]

It may subtly ruin them for clerks
this deeply involved unpickable knot of feeling
for the furred, smeared flesh of creation, the hate, the
   concern.
Viciously, out of sight, they pelt cows with stove-lengths
and hit them with pipes,
and older brothers sometimes, in more frenzied guilt,
have rancid, cracked eyes.
The city man's joke doesn't stretch to small minotaur bones.

But strange to think, as the dairy universe
reels from a Wall Street tremor, a London red-shift
on the flesh-eating graphs
and no longer only the bright and surplus children
get out of these hills,
how ghostly cows must be crowding the factory floors now
and licking black turbines
for the spectral salt
till the circuit-breaker's stunning greenhide crack
sears all but wages.

    O

In the marginal dialect of this valley
(Agen my son grows up, tourists won't hear it)
udders are *elders*.

It was very bad news for the Kirk:
old men of the hard grey cloth, their freckled faces
distended, squeezing grace through the Four Last Things
in a Sabbath bucket.
I can tell you sparetime childhoods force-fed this
make solid cheese, but often strangely veined.
I'm thinking of aunts who had telescopes to spot
pregnancies, inside wedlock or out
(there is no life more global than a village)
and my father's uncles, monsters of hospitality.

Perhaps we should forget the seven-day-week tinned bucket
and the little children dead beat at their desks
Caesar got up and Milked then he Got his soldiers –
but birds in their title work freeholds of straw
and the eagle his of sky.

Dripstone for Caesar.

The Broad Bean Sermon

Beanstalks, in any breeze, are a slack church parade
without belief, saying *trespass against us* in unison,
recruits in mint Air Force dacron, with unbuttoned leaves.

Upright with water like men, square in stem-section
they grow to great lengths, drink rain, keel over all ways,
kink down and grow up afresh, with proffered new
    greenstuff.

Above the cat-and-mouse floor of a thin bean forest
snails hang rapt in their food, ants hurry through several
    dimensions:
spiders tense and sag like little black flags in their cordage.

Going out to pick beans with the sun high as fence-tops,
    you find
plenty, and fetch them. An hour or a cloud later
you find shirtfulls more. At every hour of daylight

appear more that you missed: ripe, knobbly ones, fleshy-
    sided,
thin-straight, thin-crescent, frown-shaped, bird-shouldered,
    boat-keeled ones,
beans knuckled and single-bulged, minute green dolphins
    at suck,

beans upright like lecturing, outstretched like blessing
    fingers
in the incident light, and more still, oblique to your notice
that the noon glare or cloud-light or afternoon slants will
    uncover

till you ask yourself Could I have overlooked so many, or
do they form in an hour? unfolding into reality
like templates for subtly broad grins, like unique caught
    expressions,

like edible meanings, each sealed around with a string
and affixed to its moment, an unceasing colloquial
    assembly,
the portly, the stiff, and those lolling in pointed green
    slippers . . .

Wondering who'll take the spare bagfulls, you grin with
    happiness
– it is your health – you vow to pick them all
even the last few, weeks off yet, misshapen as toes.

The Mitchells

I am seeing this: two men are sitting on a pole
they have dug a hole for and will, after dinner, raise
I think for wires. Water boils in a prune tin.
Bees hum their shift in unthinning mists of white

bursaria blossom, under the noon of wattles.
The men eat big meat sandwiches out of a styrofoam
box with a handle. One is overheard saying:
drought that year. Yes. Like trying to farm the road.

The first man, if asked, would say *I'm one of the Mitchells.*
The other would gaze for a while, dried leaves in his palm,
and looking up, with pain and subtle amusement,

[200]

say *I'm one of the Mitchells*. Of the pair, one has been rich
but never stopped wearing his oil-stained felt hat. Nearly
  everything
they say is ritual. Sometimes the scene is an avenue.

Lachlan MacQuarie's First Language

The Governor and the seer are talking at night in a room
beyond formality. They are not speaking English.
What like were Australians, then, in the time to come?
They had lost the Gaelic in them. It had become

like a tendon a man has no knowledge of in his body
but which puzzles his bending, at whiles, with a flexing
  impulse.
They'd wide cities, dram-shops, carriages with wings –
all the visions of Dun Kenneth. The singing at a ceilidh

lacked unison, though: each man there bellowing out of him
and his eyes undirected. Had they become a nation?
They had, and a people. A verandah was their capitol
though they spoke of a town where they kept the English
  seasons.

I heard different things: a farmer was telling his son
trap rabbits and sell the skins, then you can buy your
Bugs Bunny comics! – I didn't understand this. All folk
  there,
except the child-hating ones, were ladies and gentlemen.

from *The Buladelah-Taree Holiday Song Cycle*

13.

The stars of the holiday step out all over the sky.
People look up at them, out of their caravan doors and their
    campsites;
people look up from the farms, before going back; they gaze
    at their year's worth of stars.
The Cross hangs head-downward, out there over Markwell;
it turns upon the Still Place, the pivot of the Seasons, with
    one shoulder rising:
'Now I'm beginning to rise, with my Pointers and my
    Load . . .'
hanging eastwards, it shines on the sawmills and the lakes,
    on the glasses of the Old People.
Looking at the Cross, the galaxy is over our left shoulder,
    slung up highest in the east;
there the Dog is following the Hunter; the Dog Star pulsing
    there above Forster; it shines down on the Bikies,
and on the boat-hire sheds, there at the place of the Oyster;
    the place of the Shark's Eggs and her Hide;
the Pleiades are pinned up high on the darkness, away back
    above the Manning;
they are shining on the Two Blackbutt Trees, on the rotted
    river wharves, and on the towns;
standing there, above the water and the lucerne flats, at the
    place of the Families;
their light sprinkles down on Taree of the Lebanese shops,
    it mingles with the streetlights and their glare.
People recover the starlight, hitching north,
travelling north beyond the seasons, into that country of the
    Communes, and of the Banana:
the Flying Horse, the Rescued Girl, and the Bull, burning
    steadily above that country.
Now the New Moon is low down in the west, that remote
    direction of the Cattlemen,
and of the Saleyards, the place of steep clouds, and of the
    Rodeo;

the New Moon who has poured out her rain, the moon of
    the Planting-times.
People go outside and look at the stars, and at the melon-
    rind moon,
the Scorpion going down into the mountains, over there
    towards Waukivory, sinking into the tree-line,
in the time of the Rockmelons, and of the Holiday . . .
the Cross is rising on his elbow, above the glow of the
    horizon;
carrying a small star in his pocket, he reclines there
    brilliantly,
above the Alum Mountain, and the lakes threaded on the
    Myall River, and above the Holiday.

The Grassfire Stanzas

August, and black centres expand on the afternoon
    paddock.
Dilating on a match in widening margins, they lift
a splintering murmur; they fume out of used-up grass
that's been walked, since summer, into infinite swirled
    licks.

The man imposing spring here swats with his branch,
    controlling it:
only small things may come to a head, in this settlement
    pattern.

Fretted with small flame, the aspiring islands leave
odd plumes behind. Smuts shower up every thermal
to float down long stairs. Aggregate smoke attracts a
    kestrel.

Eruption of darkness from far down under roots
is the aspect of these cores, on the undulating farmland;
dense black is withered into web, inside a low singing;
it is dried and loosened, on the surface; it is made weak.

The green feed that shelters beneath its taller death yearly
is unharmed, under new loaf soot. Arriving hawks teeter
and plunge continually, working over the hopping outskirts.

The blackenings are balanced, on a gradient of dryness
in the almost-still air, between dying thinly away
and stripping the whole countryside. Joining, they never
    gain
more than they lose. They spread away from their high
    moments.

The man carries smoke wrapped in bark, and keeps
    applying it
starting new circles. He is burning the passive ocean
around his ark of buildings and his lifeboat water;

it wasn't this man, but it was man, sing the agile
exclamatory birds, who taught them this rapt hunting
(strike! in the updrafts, snap! of hardwood pods).
Humans found the fire here. It is inherent. They learn,
wave after wave of them, how to touch the country.

Sterilizing reed distaffs, the fire edges onto a dam;
it circuits across a cow-track; new surf starts riding outward
and a nippy kestrel feeds from its foot, over cooling
    mergers.

It's the sun that is touched, and dies in expansion, mincing,
making the round dance, foretelling its future, driving
the frantic lives outwards. The sun that answers the bark tip
is discharged in many little songs, to forestall a symphony.

Cattle come, with stilted bounding calves. They look across
    the
ripple lines of heat, and shake their armed heads at them;
at random, then, they step over. Grazing smudged black
    country
they become the beasts of Tartarus. Wavering, moving out
    over
dung-smouldering ground still covered with its uncovering.

The Smell of Coal Smoke

John Brown, glowing far and down,
wartime Newcastle was a brown town,
handrolled cough and cardigan, rain on paving bricks,
big smoke to a four-year-old from the green sticks.
Train city, mother's city, coming on dark,
Japanese shell holes awesome in a park,
electric light and upstairs, encountered first that day,
sailors and funny ladies in Jerry's Fish Café.

It is always evening on those earliest trips,
raining through the tram wires where blue glare rips
across the gaze of wonderment and leaves thrilling tips.
The steelworks' vast roofed debris unrolling falls
of smoky stunning orange, its eye-hurting slump walls
mellow to lounge interiors, cut pile and curry-brown
with the Pears-Soap-smelling fire and a sense of ships
mourning to each other below in the town.

This was my mother's childhood and her difference,
her city-brisk relations who valued Sense
talking strike and colliery, engineering, fowls and war,
Brown's grit and miners breathing it, years before
as I sat near the fire, raptly touching coal,
its blockage, slick yet dusty, prisms massed and dense
in the iron scuttle, its hammered bulky roll
into the glaring grate to fracture and shoal,

its chips you couldn't draw with on the cement
made it a stone, tar crockery, different –
and I had three grandparents, while others had four:
where was my mother's father, never called Poor?
In his tie and his Vauxhall that had a boat bow
driving up the Coalfields, but where was he now?
Coal smoke as much as gum trees now had a tight scent
to summon deep brown evenings of the Japanese war,

to conjure gaslit pub yards, their razory frisson
and sense my dead grandfather, the Grafton Cornishman
rising through the night schools by the pressure in his chest
as his lungs creaked like mahogany with the grains of John
Brown.
His city, mother's city, at its starriest
as swearing men with doctors' bags streamed by toward the
docks
past the smoke-frothing wooden train that would take us
home soon
with our day-old Henholme chickens peeping in their box.

Peter Steele (1939–   )

Countdown

With hours to go before the Long Retreat –
To flameout, liftoff, hacking it with God –
The mirror has my measure. Yesterday
I fell, distracted, into the cleaving hands
Of a living barber. 'Square or normal?' was
The sum of what he asked, if you subtract
A few four-letter words, and the red-rimmed arc
Around each iris. Normal was what I asked for
As if it mattered. And now, a croppy boy,
Callan gone pudgy, a kind of cockeyed monk,
I'm framed above the basin, shaven, geared
For come-what-may tomorrow, and afraid
Afraid of death almost as much as life,
Of the bright one shearing always through the dark,
And the one, steel-jacketed, going by my name.

Element

Praying to you can be talking to the sea
Out there beyond this field, those trees
And the last tongue of land.

It is where our language ends, our dreams begin,
A world of no more world, the place
Where earth sweats into space.

And being a timid man with a taste for armour
Inside as well as out, I pray
That you will keep your distance.

Mostly it seems to work. You have the goodness
To leave me home and dry. Why then
Do I feel, unwilling, brine

In averted eyes, sweat on the folded hands,
The tongue stung as with salt, and inside
The tide mounting my veins?

Like a Ghost

An idea, like a ghost, must be spoken to a little before it will explain itself

– Dickens

Talked to the wife and children, talked to the man
Who came for the census, talked to the girl who sells
Boronia in the square, and kept on talking
To cops, to firemen, even to the priest
At a loss for words as he left the hospital:
Talked to the man arc-welding where the school
Put out new wings and bristled while the bell
Said all was over, thank you, come back soon:
Talked to the barman shrugging under spirits,
Talked to the guard while he waved the train away,
Talked to the hunchback indicating Playboy,
Talked to a bird who sheered from budding limbs,
Talked to the dog who coughed and growled dismissal,
Talked to the shuffling waves with their is and seems.
Idea, speak up: ghost me away from dreams.

Geoffrey Lehmann (1940–   )

from *Ross' Poems*

8.

You can't hear it in the house,
the wind in the upper air.
But out in the paddock
with just the sky-travelling moon
and your shadow on white grass
it sounds like a distant express train,
gusts of huge pressure,
while on the ground
the ears of phalaris are barely stirring.

My bed has a cover
of red calico striped pink.
On these cold autumn nights
grass is turning into milk,
and on the verandah where I sleep
ironbark seedlings in metal tubes
are pushing out slender blue leaves,
while down amongst the silver poplars
on a rusting mattress
the ghost of Mr Hickey sleeps.

My postal address is 'Spring Forest',
but we still talk of
'down at Hickey's'.
I wish I still had the teams
of school-pupils he used
to weed his vegetable garden
sixty years ago.
Slave labour for country schoolmasters.

The pressure lamp hisses in the kitchen,
and hot cocoa faintly steams.
A green lacewing lands on the board table.
Several times a night
Joe wakes me with her nose
to make sure I'm not dead.

The leaves of my poplars drop
into Mr Hickey's open mouth.

   28.

Driving through thick bush
alone – mist scatters in my headlights.
The death of a parent.
The earth loses its heat
by long-wave radiation at night.
When the sky is clear
the long waves go out into space,
sweltering Christmas dinners with my mother
eating her family with pudding and brandy,
stentorian gossip,
the panic in the bushfire
are leaving the earth
and shall not come back.

The earth loses its childhoods,
wood houses with their hearths
flow away into the sky,
fathers and their horses,
mothers with iron pots
are going, and wives
who were warm
when dew formed on tin roofs by the willows
leave a crater of coldness in their beds.

There are no clouds to stop them.
The long waves leave us
feeling nothing.
Movement of air in the hills
turns dew into mist.
On the plain it's dead still
getting colder and colder.
Ice grips the dust.
A frost for my mother.

37.

Some musical intervals survive
from when the ice sheets began retreating.
Feet travel over grass.

I'm travelling with a carload of calves
at night from Bega.
Shivering by the side of the road
my breath scatters over dry grass.
Trading
in the soft bones of new lives,
I come with a carload of hope
and inquisitively sniffing noses,
drink steaming coffee at a service station
under fluorescent light,
and drive on.

In colder regions (I reflect,
passing through a patch of mist)
the animals become scarcer and larger.
My tall frame is on loan
from some disgruntled ghost who lived by a peat-bog.

The farmers who will buy my calves are asleep.
Past midnight most of the lights
in the district are out.
In my back seat I carry
next year's herds
(how they'll run to meet me at the fence
and butt me in the waist) –
the latest batch from long blood-lines.

I travel through a tunnel of trees
over pale gravel,
with my lights on high beam,
the only moving object for miles.

Andrew Taylor (1940–)

Halfway to Avalon

The motor died with an underwater cough
and after a moment's gliding like a swan
and boat's beak dipped into the water's glass
and drank in stillness.
      Five miles off
the shore sketched airily where the sky began
its long arched journey over the water's bland
and plate-bald face.
      The sun climbed on
and started to coast home.
       Pinned to the tide
our hearts waited, wondered what we could do.
Could we, perhaps, stretch out a voice to where
some fisherman could catch it, haul us into shore?
Could we make love, rocking our derelict ark
back where we came from, a home hazed out of sight?
We waited and we waited, while the unseen tide
rolled over in its sleep. And when the night
flooded from the east, and evening drained
the shoreline from our hopes,
and when all but the voice
of our desperate bewilderment
drowned in the darkness, then it dawned
that this was our home, and the blindness of night
our only blanket.

Two in Search of Dawn

Black leather streets are polished by the fog
to hunting-grounds for cats, the last bus
sparkles down from the mountain, trees stretch
emptily into air. We could walk all night
and get nowhere in this winter, but the same
hacked streetwork labouring thinly toward pigeons.
Somewhere the tin thunder of a bar shutting.

Now questions issue above ground, prowling for that
satiation day withholds from them. Can we share
this foglight scurrying? We could walk
all night and practise not discovering. As it is
we walk all night, for we are both locked out.

Oh, if arms could build against the dark, refurnish it,
unpester it! But we're so far apart
we search from opposite poles of a stretched city.
It is so taut with fear, our feet drum on it,
the more anxiously we press to hunt each other
the louder night arrests us with its questions.

Jennifer Rankin (1941–79)

Williamstown

1.

The thin brown house waits with me
while the wind roughs up the bay

before us the bulk flour containers
upright on their single railway track

stand still, while at the other side
the seasky wrestles gently with the city for a line.

2. South Willie Sunday

A container ship broke some of the sky's space
just then when it sailed by up the bay,
blocking out the city that lay behind
filling my window with irregular coloured shape

now it is gone and the waves are soothing

you would not believe in boys with chequered coats
riding their rough ponies before weekend cars
not bothering to check the sea over their shoulder
or the pane of glass where I sit.

3. South Willie Tuesday

That time it was a Spaniard on a bicycle
who rode out of the bulk flour container
frame of my window, past the Magritte backdrop
where the horses graze behind the trainline yet
in front of the sea, past the telegraph pole
and the slogan slapped silos into the opposite frame

where true views of seagulls must surely begin.

4. South Willie weather

Choppy seas was the forecast yesterday.
The day before the seas were smooth.
Today you turned to me and the sea did hesitate.

Still Water Tread

Who are you to unsettle me?

Beneath this layer of water
queer white arms

dead things
left-overs pale in my bath

who are you
under the thin layers
that curl and clasp at my throat

tonight you were two arching birds
wild geese visiting my roof
learning and yearning into thickening night

you slip back
and I hear your honking
strange heavy call

my limbs linking to your voice.

Roger McDonald (1941–   )

Grasshopper

A grasshopper clings crazily
to a blade of grass,
almost upside-down,
leaning back.

Behind its wings
a man with a knapsack spray
steps closer.
Farther off

is the man's hut –
and more distant,
high up, blue ridges of basalt,
beyond them a city, the sea,

ships ploughing their small patches
of ocean. And beyond the sea
is land, a city, a blue
serration of basalt, a hut,

a man moving closer to a grasshopper, who,
leaning back, clings more crazily
and trembles on a blade of grass.

Bachelor Farmer

At half-past five – the earth cooling,
the sweat of his shirt
soaked up in red dirt –
he tunnels his arm through the weight
of a bag of wheat, slowly withdraws it,
and sees how the yellow grains
shiver, as though magnetized away
from his skin, each one alone and trembling.

Walking beside the fence, in another paddock,
he discovers a grain
caught in the hairs of his wrist;
he bends down, allows it to fall,
and with the careful toe of his boot
presses it into the ground.

All night sprawled on the verandah of his hut,
he wakes to the call of the pallid cuckoo,
its blunted scale
low on the heads of unharvested wheat –

not rising towards him, not falling away,
but close by, unchanging, incomplete.

Others

Who of those asleep at midnight over blank television
    screens,
or drunk in the brooding city,
or hands in pockets staring through glass at black trees, at
    stars,
would believe when the gate has clicked,
the tail-light swayed red,
the exhaust purred catlike down a hollow,
that these who turn-in closing the safe door,
who climb under blankets mountainous as coal,
listen – while night unfurls through frosty boulders –
to the long deliberation of wood, cold roofing iron,
and wait for the earth to crack, itself beneath them turning
    cold
and unvaried; this contemplation turning them out to stare
hands in pockets through glass, at stars,
listening late to the slow degrees of alteration in their lives.

John Tranter (1943–   )

Sonnet 63 from *Crying in Early Infancy*

In a distant field, small animals prepare
for sleep, under the huge rising moon.
For foreign peasants, dusk is none too soon.
The bombers fade into the melting air.
In a far harbour boats make for their mooring,
in another town the citizens are glad
the lights are going out. The morning's bad,
the waiting news is cruel, the job boring.

A painter pours a cheap and bitter drink
and drinks it down. His hand's unsteady;
on the table brush and pen and ink
lie scattered. Half his work's no good,
the rest is sold for rent. He's ready;
the loaded gun discharges as it should.

Butterfly

When she was fourteen, she says,
she ran away from home, at sixteen
she bought a big bike and hit the road,
moving from town to town, looking for
something she can't explain.
Later, with her fluffy blonde hair
tucked under a cap, she worked at
fixing computers for a living.
It's just one weird thing after another;
an odd life, she says, for a farmer's daughter.

Now, briefly, she's alighted
behind the counter of the aquarium shop
to wait out the winter. We sit and talk
while the fish gape and kiss the glass
in a bother of colourless bubbles.
Her blue eyes are wide awake and dreaming:
she's inside a huge television set
under the sea, surrounded by a movie
of a coral reef where a million
coloured fish flicker like confetti.
She shows me the book she's reading:
see, she says, when a butterfly
breaks out of the cocoon, it is already
delicate and pretty.
She lights another cigarette, stares out
through the rainy window at the street
full of showers and the heavy traffic
stalled on the hill,
thinking of the open road,
sunshine, and the next flower.

At the Criterion

I don't go to the pub much any more –
they pulled down the Newcastle ten years ago,
and the Forest Lodge is full of young punks
who can't hold their drink. But now and then –
say, some Friday night when my room
gets on my nerves, with its endless books,
with the pool of lamplight on the table,
the traffic outside my window,
the crowds, the rush and babble, then,
just for old times' sake, I go out.
And she's sure to be there, in the corner bar,
laughing with that young executive
who goes down to the snow in the winter
and has a town house in Double Bay.

They look happy enough. He seems
quite at ease and familiar with her,
though he's only known her a few months –
does he know yet, for example,
that she had an abortion two years ago,
at seventeen, and still isn't over it?
That her mother won't speak to her now
because of the 'immoral things' she did
with her pretty room-mate at College;
that she likes Seafood Avocado, and can't stand
cats, or poverty; and when she makes love
with that awkward desperation, sad and hurried –
at that peak of moaning frenzy
brief tears gather in her eyes: she's not crying,
not happy, just 'a bit out of it', as she says.
Well, he'll learn these things, if he's
attentive, and if it lasts long enough.
Even now – and I'm only on my seventh drink –
she's paying rather too much attention to that
academic type near the door – an older man,
good-looking in a rough sort of way;
a drunk, but with a charming line of talk.
And she prefers older men.
                              When I've had enough
I'll go back to the flat and pour a scotch
and read over my notes on Cavafy –
a Greek poet, dead long ago,
who lived very fast when he was young
then spent a lonely middle age remembering
his youth in Alexandria, the sordid affairs . . .
patiently sketching a portrait of his
beautiful, corrupt and much-loved city –
'its fever, its absolute devotion to pleasure'.

Robert Adamson (1944–   )

Action Would Kill It / A Gamble

for Keith Hull, 1966

When I couldn't he always discussed things.
His talk drew us together;
the government's new war, the best french brandies
and breaking the laws. And it seemed
a strange thing for us to be doing;
the surf right up the beach, wetting our
feet each wave.

On that isolated part of the Coast, counting over
the youngest politicians.
Huge shoulders of granite grew higher
as we walked on, cutting us from perspectives.
He swung his arms and kicked
lumps of quartz hard with bare feet, until I asked
him to stop it . . .

He didn't care about himself at all, and the sea
just licked his blood away.
The seemingly endless beach held us firm;
we walked and walked all day
until it was dark. The wind dropped off and the surf
flattened out, as silence grew round
us in the darkness.

We moved on, close together almost touching;
he wouldn't have noticed, our
walk covered time rather than distance.
When the beach ended,
we would have to split up. And as he spoke
clearly and without emotion
about the need for action, about killing people,
I wanted him.

[223]

Wade in the Water

When all the rivers turn back again in our time
to cavernous orange tracks
trailing aimless through the country

new animals bumping rocks in the moonlight
will remind us of their search
for watercourses that tumble to sea

even into our dreams their pursuit continues
and watching a chemical glow
beam from caves we will not dream

even truth raised in sadness will not help us
in school playgrounds
among jokes about grammarians

or teachers explaining the empty caskets

Clean air will be breathed in by our children
for their pointless laughter

farmers will not remember the trade names
of their fathers' poisons
and the new animals will move about carefully in moonlight

taking it in like students

My Granny

When my Granny was dying
I'd go into her bedroom
and look at her

she'd tell me to get out of it
leave this foul river

it will wear you out too

she was very sick
and her red curly hair
was matted and smelt of gin

sometimes I sat there all day
listening to the races
and put bets on for her at the shop

and I sat there the afternoon
she died and heard her say her last words
and I sat there not telling

maybe three hours
beside the first dead person I'd seen

I tried to drink some of her gin
it made me throw up on the bed
and then I left her

she said the prawns will eat you
when you die on the Hawkesbury River

My First Proper Girlfriend

The first girl I wanted to marry
was Joan Hunter
her father owned more oyster leases
than anyone else on the river

she had buck teeth
but she looked okay really

we'd sit on her father's wharf
and watch the mullet together for hours

they will take over the world one day

we loved each other alright

my parents hated us being together
and called her Bugs Bunny

One night my father cut Joan's Dad
with a fishing knife
right down his left cheek

that little protestant bludger
with his stuck-up bitch of a daughter

from *Growing Up Alone*

11.

Fishing skiff in the light
at Mackerel Flats, mud-caked, sun borne
by the old man caulking cracks.

Rust scales drop from boat-slip
to silt as he moves.

Gnawed, hacked heads of black bream
rock through the wash.

Skeleton trophies, Banjo Rays,
staked out on a pile,
their whip tails, paralyzed chalk.

Light seeps through
the folds of his turky neck –
his eyes don't blink

and flick out involuntarily to where
mud-gudgers pick at the heads.

He is alone with his tinkering work,
he holds the scraper
like a little axe and chips
away at the belly of his boat.

His finger flesh grown over
his finger nails, his hair freckled white,
his pupils contracted points.

It is morning
and the mangrove air is sweet

as I move toward him
my leather cracking oyster grit.

I ask how's the fishing

my alien voice reminding me

he is the grandfather of what I am.

My Afternoon

I think of sex all afternoon

it becomes memory
the wide beds
and the fleshy women

who got me here

the mornings are best
spent alone
I can't do anything in the mornings
with women anymore

I am taken from place to place
as I pretend
to be good about sex

then quite drunk
I lie back in the folds
of their particular sheets

face buried in fear near shame

Robert Gray (1945–   )

Journey: the North Coast

Next thing, I wake up in a swaying bunk,
as though on board a clipper
lying in the sea,
and it's the train, that booms and cracks,
it tears the wind apart.
Now the man's gone
who had the bunk below me. I swing out,
cover his bed and rattle up the sash –
there's sunlight teeming
on the drab carpet. And the water sways
solidly in its silver basin, so cold
it joins together through my hand.
I see from where I'm bent
one of those bright crockery days
that belong to so much I remember.
The train's shadow, like a bird's,
flees on the blue and silver paddocks,
over fences that look split from stone,
and banks of fern,
a red clay bank, full of roots,
over a dark creek, with logs and leaves suspended,
and blackened tree trunks.
Down these slopes move, as a nude descends a staircase,
slender white gum trees,
and now the country bursts open on the sea –
across a calico beach, unfurling;
strewn with flakes of light
that make the whole compartment whirl.
Shuttering shadows. I rise into the mirror
rested. I'll leave my hair
ruffled a bit that way – fold the pyjamas,
stow the book and wash bag. Everything done,

press down the latches into the case
that for twelve months I've watched standing out
of a morning, above the wardrobe
in a furnished room.

A Kangaroo

That hungry face
moves on grass
the way an artist's pencil
retouches
shadows.

Then, when he's bounding
The head's borne
refined as a deer's, relaxed,
before
a powerful tight basketball attack.

And the toe-nail, in the fore-front,
a stevedore's claw
(tears with it, cantilevered on his tail);
the forepaws
are a housedog's, begging.

So that here,
sitting up and simply, is the unknown
energy, which is nature,
that's able to spawn, as one,
every extreme thing.

'The Single Principle of Forms'

All day a storm has fermented. Now the clouds are huge
above the mountains.
A horse stands in the paddock and swings its wooden
face at the flies.
It stands with one hind-leg poised lightly by the other,
like the way a male ballet dancer stands.
Its muzzle soggy as the stump of a freshly-cut banana
palm.
And that coarse long tail makes you think of an Indian,
waiting with a tomahawk amongst the forest.
The horse trembles its flank in the heat, and now
lightning shudders –
A silverish lightning, over those great haunches of
cloud.

North Coast Town

Out beside the highway, first thing in the morning,
nothing much in my pockets but sand
from the beach. A Shell station (with their Men's locked),
a closed hamburger stand.

I washed at a tap down beside the changing sheds,
stepping about on mud. Through the wall
smell of the vandals' lavatory,
and an automatic chill flushing in the urinal.

Eat a floury apple, and stand about. At this kerb
sand crawls by, and palm fronds here
scrape dryly. Car after car now – it's like a boxer
warming-up with the heavy bag, spitting air.

A car slows and I chase it. Two hoods
going shooting. Tattoos and the greasy Fifties pompadour.
Rev in High Street, drop their first can.
Plastic pennants on this distilled morning, everywhere;

a dog trotting, and someone hoses down a pavement;
our image flaps in shop fronts; smoking on
past the pink 'Tropicana' motel (stucco, with sea-shells);
the RSL, like a fancy-dress Inca; the 'Coronation',

a warehouse picture show. We pass
bulldozed acres. The place is becoming chrome,
tile-facing, and plate-glass: they're making California.
Pass an abo, not attempting to hitch, outside town.

The Sea-Shell

White as crockery,
it stands on the ledge of the long verandah window
in a white plank wall.

The trellis-lights –
negative, scrap shapes – are swung in here stiffly
as torch beams.

The shell is a lifting spinnaker.
And close-up, there are patterns in beige,
similar to a feather's.

The shell is wound
the same as pastry, and it has that same decorative
ruffled edging.

Coloured lead inserts in these bare windows.
Vine-patterns are stirring. Conifers,
bird movements. A Sunday.

The sound in the shell
is that of the whole Order at their evening meal,
along dim passages, behind doors.

The shell is cool, remote;
its shape causes a peristalsis in your palm,
it is breast-tipped.

Closed, adamant shell –
you think of some girl, who has been waited for here;
who's come, at last, from church;

who is received in her cool,
coiffured whiteness. Like the shell,
underneath her that dark passage, and damp smell.

Sketch of the Harbour

The long, wet trajectory of the ferry's railing
widely outswinging
is safely caught in my hand.

And I watch a yacht that is coasting by,
at its bow the fuming
of a champagne bottle's lip.

All about on the harbour the yachts are slowly waltzing,
or in close-up
their ecstatic geometry.

Light fragments crackling above the suburbs and water,
whitely, as from a welder's torch,
on a soap-white day.

In the shadow of the ferry, the oily, dense water
is flexile, striated
as launching muscles.

But further out, there is only sunlight over a surface –
a constant flickering, like a lit-up
airport control.

And the gulls, white as flying foam, lie beside us here
with clear balloons of air
underneath their arms.

Landscape

After the tide's long gear-shifting gesture
glimpsed among the bush,
climbing down toward ocean shallows'
tilting opalescence.

A washed sandbar, the yellow of a melon;
rocks' wet terracotta;
a viridescent cloud,
sponge-pitted, that is crinkled weeds –

these are somewhere underneath the sluice
of cellophane-clear,
fast-drawn-off-the-roller, billowing
water, light-glistened.

Leaning above this, out of rock, angophoras –
flesh-pink clamber
all over the dense, ink blueness of the sky.
Trees like Schiele's posturings.

And two of them clash, their shadows clamped on
a single stone – leaping for the sun
with fingertips
that basketball players try to grow.

Christine Churches (1945–   )

Neighbour

I know him only as a man of Sunday afternoon, and a
                        backyard fire burning.
There, by the flame-tree, the man is stooping and brooding;

He feeds on the flames and the armfuls of smoke
which he can create with his old bent hoe;
he is content, and she is silent; enough that he is working.

There, by the flame-tree;
smoke sulks and powders from the parasite flame,
greys and ashes the hard-muscled tree;
the man is stooping and bending:
dull, pleasing pokes of the hoe,
the flame clings hold of the stubborn leaves.
He suns his thoughts,
there, by the flame-tree,
with the flowers of filleting scarlet,
too soon unjoined from the flowing branches;
raking up the leaves and the loosely jointed twigs,
and burning them, stubbornly, with those of his mind.

I know him only as a man of Sunday afternoon, and a
                        backyard fire burning;
so who shall ever know him, and all his unburnt thoughts;
which the good-wife watching from the window
                        must never know or see?

Divination

Bottle-brush is best, it likes sweet water;
burning in shallow lamps of land,
densely wired scarlet incandescent among leaves.
A twig can read the entrails of the earth:
prophesy with forked stick
that bends like a snake to the flicker of water.
Trap the place with a pile of stones.

Water for cattle, they camp by its side;
breathe out slow blessings
when they bend to drink.
Bottle-brush is best; spilling
bright water: earth
slit to the bone.

Late Summer Storm

Angry-feathered trees,
stiff-winged quills of rocking rage;
cockatoos caught in a banker of storm,
trees dumped out in the air,
tight-hanging birds and a tangle of branches panting
    behind.

The sky flaps clear of ruin,
shaken river runs back into light,
slapping the boats in a panic for air.
Bare flat earth gleams with sudden grown mud,
and we swim in the water still warm after rain.

Grandmother's Ninetieth Birthday

We cover the hole in the ground
with cake and candles,
brightly coloured table-cloths
and a cluster of solemn balloons.

It is a gathering of strong chins
and large Cornish ears.
The backs of the old men still shaped
to the tunnel's crouch,
the women humped as cottage chimneys.

One day soon
we will dig back through the ninety layers of earth
that cover her life,
prise out an era of fossils.
Lace antimacassars pressed thin as fern,

petticoats crimped into fluted shells,
apron bright as chapel white-wash.
A stubborn Cornish life
embedded in layers of rock and silted clay.

We arrange her carefully at the table of honour,
neat as the exhibit in a Folk museum.
Good for another twenty years we praise her;
but the sound of grown men singing around her
is the candle bright as fire-lit copper
that will light her into the ground.

I Wonder What Went of Him

Twisting words into slow shape,
rolling them over and over,
licking them tight
as home-made cigarettes
tucked up behind each ear.

We stop by for a yarn,
he's drilling for water.
Hat shoved forward, or
lifted clear; a rock pulled up from a nest of slaters,
the ditch of sunless flesh
swarming with moisture.

     There's oil down there.
     Did I tell you about Charley?
     Always catching rabbits with grease on their ears;
     gets grease for all his tractors now
     – straight from that burrer.
     There's oil alright.

We shove shoulder to shoulder,
dodge and trick our shadows around the hole.
A piece of broken mirror
drops a lighted flare of sunlight
down the shaft –
a jet of fire,
striking it rich

with one bright eye of water
winking up from the earth.

Walking in the Lambing Paddock

That Spring I was twelve
the lambs were shattered from the nursery plate,
sprawled in the dust like shivering phlegm

or choked halfway
the legs stuck out like saucepan handles.
I was running for help

but the lamb lay dead, folded flat
as a sheet to be put in the cupboard,
and the ewe with the wool

peeled clean from her skin
floats in the paddock
like a lost balloon.

Dry branches dragged slowly
seed a trail of brittle leaves
criss-crossed in heaps

and set alight
with the flames' slow prickle
like the tears on my face.

Rhyll McMaster (1947–   )

Slanted World

I rose to catch the early morning,
the different japanee-painted world of six a.m.
The chilled sunlight in long, uneasy fingers
stretched across the terrace,
snatching at the zithered goldfish sucking at dew drops
by the pond's cement edge.
They swam to goggle at my dabbling finger, quirked
like a magnified, nail-headed worm,
then tucked away, giving disappointed, air gasping
suck-suck-burrpps.

I sat quiet, waiting for the geta slap, slap
sound of the doves as they crash landed in the pines;
then turned to watch the glistening crow
settled in the branches of the blossomed peach –
he knew the pink became him.

Soon an eastern wind shivered round my feet
and made a ruffled path in the duck weed on the pond –
The goldfish rose to catch the stir, their pale,
water-honey sides like through-water-seen tin.

Another world lies
in my garden – for me to see through slanted eyes;
I walk with care in the strange-world orient atmosphere of
     six a.m.
where, surfacing to bubble-break their silver ceiling
the careless goldfish laugh.

Fire Screen

Frost on the ground,
black earth touched with silent gold;
cold beaten brass stare of the two foxes
in the screen shielding the fireplace.

The small one snatches a scent,
back bent in a much bolder
quivering stance than the other
who muzzle up, caught out, guilty-glanced,
holds the moon on his shoulder.

Colder and colder, caught forever
as if in the glare of the gunman's lamp;
I wish they'd been shot, those foxes,
that scared me as a child;

such wild fear that they'd catch
the naked wooden statue of the kneeling girl
to leave startled splinters on the mantel.

I'm older now, my fear's locked away
in one of those secret boxes;
often don't have to check the kneeling girl stays whole –
though you can't be sure with foxes
for sometimes when the door blocks the light
I hear their necks crack as they turn and watch.

Bird of Glass

Do you remember the peacocks
that screamed from the Gardens behind our beach house?
In the mornings
above the sea noise they would shriek, thin as silver,
sharp and viridescent as lettuce
and the old, one-eyed
emu would play mocker with his drum-thud.

It still reaches to the present;
but those peacocks' ringed feathers
are dull as brown soil mud,
tarnished as the pennies in our game of shops
that clinked down the stair rail
between rows of pins.

What a young child I was
to think those summers could be held under
a glass bell;
I spun a metal thread between thumb and finger
and was not cut.

Remember we played
Leap and Run with each other on the sandhills
till we leapt into dark?
We were like that photograph
of the sinewed negro children
caught mid-air, laughs frozen.

Who will go back?
A drag-hemmed lady
conducting echoes from a park rotunda
sees the Council workmen coming,
each with an axe;
Her eyes fill as they hack at the floor boards
and her skirt seems to cling with a child's fingers
as some loose threads catch.

Dream in an Afternoon

Lying with my back on the slanted weir
I cannot press my feet hard enough
on the hot cement and stone.
I reach over and you
are at arm's distance.
In this short dream in an afternoon we are as one
as two people ever want.
We watch beneath dropped eyelids
the small, light-catching fish go giddying past;
Yet I know the end of afternoon will come;

Raise up on a warmth-weak elbow
man in a green jumper,
lean over and block the sky,
for frowning, I see over your left shoulder
small as Silvereyes
two bright dirigibles drift towards the sun.

A Dream of Washed Hair

Standing under the shower
my mother washes her hair;
she is small and young.
She slicks back her hair from the temples
with the palm of one hand.
Her skin looks secret and cool;
her life does not go on from here.

Though she dresses and goes
this I don't see in my dream;
she leans and smiles.
She is not thinking of me
though I stare in her eyes.
She is thinking of nothing at all
in that water, this dream, that stopped world.

Washing the Money

At weekends, my father and younger sister
scrubbed the Queen's obdurate lips in the bathroom basin
where plain soap, warm water
made money a clean creation.
The silk grease of pounds, maroon tint of 'fivers',
the crisper starch of a ten shilling note
snapped and capered under his fingertips.

I saw millions of unmatched fingerprints,
bone transparent, brittle snail shells
bump around the rim.
Nothing strange in washing the currency
which lay exhausted like strained, wet cabbage.

Then they ironed it dry between best linen tea towels
while my mother hovered, grim;
'Oh darl,' she said, 'don't singe them.'
Puffs of rich steam jumped up
over that pair of alchemists' shoulders
who, oblivious, never asked
if she meant the tea towels or the money.

Seven in the Morning

In here it's seven o'clock.
Out over the Pacific light hangs
in the white corner of a sheet of cloud.
I can just make out the figure of a woman bent down.
Her hair's blown;
strings of brown seaweed whip past.

From last night's rain
the sand is pocked and gouged.
There's the scent of crabs or mud.
The ocean swell is too full
lumping this way, that, pickling sharks.

Behind the house light green seagrass
gives off a curry smell
that butts dully with the air.
Next door the paper gets delivered
with a stuffed thud.
The woman's disappeared.
Two streets back a dog yaps, another barks.

Eeling

Pearlised shadows
under the Tilley lamp.
Nothing.
Only river phlegm, a serpenty masquerade.

Short, grey, luminous snouts.
Intelligent dogs' heads
that weave and sneak into rock crevices.
Pinned down with tridents
they mimic water currents.
Bashed with their own camouflage
of stones, thrashed with sticks,
exhorted to give up
the struggle and die.

Die you slippery bastard!
Noting the truth about eels firsthand.
Three in the bag still ticking.
Six get away through water and eel grass,
land-rushing, doubling back;
marine foxes.

Carrying back small cauldrons
of eel country
blood-warm in our boots,
through the stumble of night paddocks;
mouths watering.

Martin Johnston (1947–1990)

Aristarchus and the Whale

Let us, to pass the time as we cycle
to where we'll fish, retell
the old, old tale we used to love hearing
at bedtime or in Sunday-school
of how, persecuted by the tyrant Polycrates
for building bicycles without a licence,
Aristarchus of Samos, on the advice
of his old tutor Pythagoras (now something
high up in the corridors of power),
took refuge in the great fish
until, centuries later, it was caught
by several fishermen simultaneously
(another story, that)
to the immense and justified alarm
of Polycrates, who had read
in an old almanac (he was, poor fellow,
superstitious) that should something of the sort
occur, he was in for
a nasty end, and had consequently adopted
the alias of 'Urban VIII' (and wore for protection
a signet-ring stamped with a fish),
none of which helped him, bicycles
emerging from the whale's maw in endless implacable
     streams
having rolled over and over him ever since,
while Aristarchus' subsidiaries,
under a variety of names,
have taken out floods of patents
on up-to-date systems of gears;
let us by all means retell the old tale
even if, when younger, we may have
misinterpreted the moral. Ah,
but the one that got away!

The Scattering Layer

Rain walks all night across the greenhouse roof
on awkward spike-footed stilts, and in the yard, where
     weeds
and furtive clothespegs interweave, it smears
bluegreen on appleblue leafmould frottage, snaps open
galls where grubs gleam and wrinkle, silverfoil
uncurling waterfalls among the twigs, and cats stare up at
     the stickman.
The stock-car races slide across the compass,
lurch with a crunch and glass breaking up against the end
     of the street,
burglars are picked out in light on the doorsteps, even
     primroses
glow, and the wingcases of dazed beetles. There are chalk
     diagrams but what goes on
up beyond the Van Allen belt, the scattering layer,
we're not sure: pick up glittering striations, unreadable
     patterns of dots
in the strepitant blueblack undersea rivers, krill or seedspill
raining on us, down here where we swirl in our own light.

Michael Dransfield (1948–73)

Pioneer Lane

Erskineville. The sun came round a corner,
and saw, and went. The sun's habitual corner.
Nothing unusual. The air they breathe
rolls out obscenely from the factory chimneys.
Old age. Just that. No more. And an appraisal
of work-years wasting in these sunless narrows
of terrace-streets which close themselves away,
rejecting newness like the baby stifled
by Leagues Club widows and the warm indifference
of public bars, and traffic loud and poisonous.
Day is so stale; sit in the sun; let it
warm away your questions. Things seem better
in the sun, even when you are old,
as old as these – or so we think – or almost.
Their retribution comes beyond the grave.
Not savage or pretentiously hostile,
they'll gather round, these veterans of Lone Pine
and Villers-Bret. and Passchendaele and Ypres,
a circle close with friendship; and there'll be
no pension-degradation; they'll be free,
these pioneers who made Australia
and fought to keep it, time on bitter time,
a place they could grow old in, never thinking
they'd be despised for even that senescence.
They think I know, of those who stayed behind
in the warm ridges of Gallipoli,
or Flanders mud. A cigarette-smoke circle,
two coins tossed high into the endless year,
falling to choruses of 'Jesus Christ'.

The Grandfather

for J.M.S.

inside the gates his drive is a chain of ponds. the car stalls,
we walk the rest of the way. arriving at his verandah
we are met by green relatives, scented, waving, touching
    us.
he pushes the door, which falls open; no-one and footsteps.

the land he holds is time's reward. bare, wily trees take
    over,
cling for a living to the stone, and orchids
wild in an echo stable.

he tells the story of the ghost; we dine; outside, the wind
catches the high, rusted sails of a windmill which cries
red dust in dimming air. crows rise from a roof, it is time to
    go.

back in the city, the middle of a week, none of him
seems real. the house, thousands of acres gone to seed,
    would be
his flying ship which turned to stone, a girl
he visits instead of dying, his Dutchman's port of call.

Presences

at last the night comes, stifling the sun
with horizons, a hangman's drop,
steps for the thirteen hours of today. above the roofs
    something
like a bitten eye races the bombers home, to their
black fields and iron houses. uneasily
some stars come, our jewelled neighbours, cold
as a distance, as a loss. the other side of darkness
is where she lives, the
land and sea and land away.
her kiss is a postmark and her voice
sounds along wire. we meet
on week-old pages like clichés. but
around her bed and mine, I know the same
winter steals, which chills the body and makes
air a frozen moat, and objects islands, and
which is not winter.

John Forbes (1950–)

Rolling in Money

Flexed suddenly the muscles of the stomach
can make the joints in the back of the neck
go 'crack'. This clears the room for you,
like a pirouette, full of energy but passive,
the way these diaries of pure sensation
balance your responses against how you think
you will respond, leaving a margin of wind
for you to turn into. Not actually a repeat
performance, but more like an encore from
where you will collapse completely. Nothing
or no one will pass you by, just as a body
lying on the floor is probably not dead but
really relaxed in a total trance, so the rise &
fall of your chest arches over the day-to-day
posture you impose / on appearing as you are
– that is, not really knowing you're alive
until the air touches more than your idea of
its following you around. Instead you are
in the wake of the air, preceding your first
impressions: delicate & quick, but here left
out of things, like a law of karma that will
never improve you. Just as a dead calm will
never delay the Owl & the Pussycat in their
beautiful pea-green boat, so you will continue
breathing like a sail & the comic loot from
this effect piles up on the deck; lots of money &
plenty of honey, wrapped up in a five-pound note.

Blonde & Aussie

Boosting the hula hoop, fates
are gala ridden but aware the
best detectives swallow dice.

Who aims at a bunch of lakes?
A tree carved to a pencil the
breeze steadies like a degree?

It trembles but delivers. And
a drought breaks after cloud-
seeding Dawn opens her blouse

and hears another 'classical'
epithet: 'wine-ruined sinus', a
harmony that defects & later

a dancer imagines it. The balance
we have abolished is prinked
& a spoon bangs on a basin

because a baby grabs it. His
arm moves like a coda to sleep:
allow impulse status, the upper

deck tilts at the risk banjo
music poses. For us it atrophies
the way whistle stops disrupt

barn-storming. Or a cute belt
of whisky slops in a tin cup.
Vitamins, rinse out that drink!

Kevin Hart (1954–   )

A Dream of France

Restless at night and during storms
my father tore me from my heavy sleep

like a picture from a thick black book –
and walked me through his dream,

the nightmare streets of 1944
that stuck him to the past.

He groped about my room, barefoot,
unearthly, gasping as shells

unleashed their violet energy
about his hugeness, then

quietly curled up on my bed
one eye half-open, waiting

for the dark to come upon him
as a picture when the page is turned.

This Day

The clock above stalled traffic, white as bread;
women, serving time, spilling out from factories;
my Grandfather breathing in sawdust like pepper;

Greek women in black, like olives; men in bars
watching their drinks begin to watch them back:
this day, a compass pointing in all directions.

Newspapers with headlines like ink-blot tests;
a red telephone, ringing, as if boiling over:
this day, a flame burning inside each one of us.

Mosquitoes humming like a tuning-fork just struck;
the moon, the sun's disguise; girls dressed to kill –
and thoughts, like sharpened knives, behind the eye.

This day, sometimes a ship, sometimes an ocean:
that man who wears his dead wife's wedding-ring;
the clock above the darkened city, like a host.

Keys turned in locks; grease wiped from chins;
the strange rituals of those who believe in death.
This day, done with, like a nail hit once and bent.

Midsummer

These are the richest weeks
when light slows to heat, when all that grows
fattens with the sweetest juices –
and the cloudless sky
so heavy, as though we walked through cloud.

Green summer has come –
and you are dressed in white.
Simply to be here, now, in the heat's stunned silence
with all of time ahead, to think of it
as something given, a garden.

Forget the listless nights,
the darkness that will not accept our roots,
the wasp among the poppies,
the soldiers marching past the orchard.
Our day is here, today,

and even tomorrow has begun
though far away from us, in cities still cold,
in grasping hands,
in rooms where spiders dream of lace.
It will be all that was promised,

tomorrow, the new land,
as though I have never touched you before:
another day, as rich as this,
the garden in blossom, the river's hush, the promise
renewed through change: this world.

The Real World

Rays of sunlight quietly fishing from tall trees;
a wrestler, smoking, his fingers fat as toes;
old men in bars, with arms that end in glass;
a haloed moon tonight, a hole within a hole.

Steel factories like German concentration camps;
the orchestra, tuning, mixing its new palette;
Myers deserted at night, a museum from the future;
and tying shoelaces, a hole that's through a hole.

Rain pecking at the window-pane; a dripping star
that took a thousand years to find this lake;
a discotheque bulging with mirrors and music;
a black hole, a hole in space, that hole.

The cutting-blade of sunlight shaving Africa;
pipe-smoke curling slowly upwards, a cobra's ghost;
the child's black pupil with its coffin's shine.
And a hole within a hole that's through a hole.

Your Shadow

At daylight
it is already obsessed,
wearing black as if expecting your funeral
and trying to be a grave.

All morning the sun tries to distract,
displaying mountains, offering flowers,
then, furious,
burns it within an inch of life
at noon, when it crawls in under your feet.

But watch: it returns
vast, superior, freshened by failure and rest,
and noses ahead of you like a dog
or lags behind,
sprawling on the pavement peering up dresses.

It sees you as fat, dwarfish, beneath contempt;
and, dreaming of victory,
stretches its long tentacles to others, pulling
until your last strength goes.

Your only hope:
turn on a light, quickly,
then, a fisherman, you can hold a slithering catch
like this strange thing
still clambering to get out my window –
defeated,
though not for long.

Come Back

Come back to me.
The road is waiting quietly outside your door,
the wind is blowing the leaves this way.
It is late afternoon,
the best time for making love; half the world
is sleeping now: no longer sad
the violins fit
into their velvet cases, and lovers there
must do without their eyes.

Come back. I want to tell you how
all of the things I only half-believed before
are true, I want to find
that part of you I never touched
and make it blossom,
I want the clock to count the hours as seconds
until your sorrow is forgotten.

Come back.
Don't watch the sunlight lazing on the street,
don't wait for fruit to grow without a rind.
You know the way,
the heat that's in the flesh by afternoon,
the taste of salt,
the face that fits into your eyes.
I want to know, again,
what it's like to breathe your words;
I want to know, once more,
how it feels
to be peeled and eaten whole, time after time.

Acknowledgements

We are indebted to the copyright holders for permission to reprint certain poems:

ROBERT ADAMSON: 'Action Would Kill It/A Gamble', 'Wade in the Water', 'My Granny', 'My First Proper Girlfriend', *from* 'Growing Up Alone', and 'My Afternoon', by permission of the author; BRUCE BEAVER: *from* 'Letters to Live Poets' and *from* 'Lauds and Plaints' from *Selected Poems*, copyright © Bruce Beaver 1979, by permission of Collins/ Angus & Robertson Publishers, Australia and South Head Press, Australia; JOHN BLIGHT: 'Cormorants' and 'Mangrove' from *Selected Poems 1939–1975*, copyright © John Blight 1976, by permission of Collins/Angus & Robertson Publishers, Australia; 'Conflagration' and 'The Disarrayed' from *Pageantry for a Lost Empire*, copyright © John Blight 1977, by permission of Collins/Angus & Robertson Publishers, Australia; VINCENT BUCKLEY: 'Death in January', *from* 'Golden Builders', 'The Blind School', 'Your Father's House' and 'Internment' from *Selected Poems*, copyright © The Estate of Vincent Buckley 1981, by permission of Collins/Angus & Robertson Publishers, Australia; 'Teaching German Literature' by permission of Penelope Buckley; DAVID CAMPBELL: 'Men in Green', 'Who Points the Swallow', *from* 'Works and Days', *from* 'Starting from Central Station', 'Sugar Loaf', 'Landfall', 'Portents over Coffee' and *from* 'Two Songs with Spanish Burdens' from *Collected Poems*, copyright © Judith Campbell 1989, by permission of Collins/Angus & Robertson Publishers, Australia; CHRISTINE CHURCHES: 'Neighbour', 'Divination' and 'Late Summer Storm' from *My Mother and The Trees*, copyright © Christine Churches, by permission of Collins/ Angus & Robertson Publishers, Australia; 'Grandmother's Ninetieth Birthday', 'I Wonder What Went of Him' and 'Walking in the Lambing Paddock', by permission of the author; ALEXANDER CRAIG: 'The Ceiling' and 'The Bottles',

'In the Park', 'Dust to Dust' and 'Winter Quarters' from
Selected Poems, copyright © Gwen Harwood 1975, by
permission of Collins/Angus & Robertson Publishers,
Australia; 'Looking towards Bruny', 'Dialogue' and 'Mother
Who Gave Me Life' from *The Lion's Bride*, copyright ©
Gwen Harwood 1981, by permission of Collins/Angus &
Robertson Publishers, Australia; A. D. HOPE: 'Easter Hymn',
'The Gateway', 'Ascent into Hell' (with dedication)' 'The
Pleasures of Princes', 'The Death of the Bird', 'The Coasts of
Cerigo', 'Advice to Young Ladies', 'Lament for the
Murderers' and 'Loving Kind' from *Collected Poems 1930–
1970*, copyright © A. D. Hope 1966, 1969, 1972, by
permission of Collins/Angus & Robertson Publishers,
Australia; 'Inscription for a War', from *Antechinus Poems*,
copyright © A. D. Hope 1981, by permission of Collins/
Angus & Robertson Publishers, Australia; MARTIN
JOHNSTON: 'Aristarchus and the Whale' and 'The Scattering
Layer' from *The Typewriter Considered as a Bee-Trap* (1984), by
permission of Hale & Ironmonger Pty Ltd, Australia; EVAN
JONES: 'A Solicitors' World' from *Left at the Post* (1984), by
permission of University of Queensland Press; 'The Falling
Sickness', 'Hostel', 'A Line from Keats' and 'Honeymoon,
South Coast' from *Understandings*, by permission of the
author; GEOFFREY LEHMANN: from *Ross' Poems*, copyright ©
Geoffrey Lehmann 1978, by permission of Collins/Angus &
Robertson Publishers, Australia; JAMES MCAULEY:
'Dialogue', 'Jesus', 'The Tomb of Heracles', 'Father, Mother,
Son', 'Against the Dark' and 'One Tuesday in Summer'
from *Collected Poems 1936–70*, copyright © Norma McAuley
1971, by permission of Collins/Angus & Robertson
Publishers, Australia; 'Autumn in Hobart' and 'Parish
Church', by permission of Curtis Brown (Aust) Pty Ltd;
ROGER MCDONALD: 'Grasshopper', 'Bachelor Farmer' and
'Others' from *Airship* (1975), by permission of University of
Queensland Press; KENNETH MACKENZIE: 'The Snake',
'Caesura', 'Two Trinities' and 'An Old Inmate' from *The
Poems of Kenneth Mackenzie*, copyright © E. Little and H. S.
Mackenzie 1972, by permission of Collins/Angus &
Robertson Publishers, Australia; RHYLL MCMASTER: 'Slanted

[261]

copyright © Elizabeth Riddell 1989, by permission of
Collins/Angus & Robertson Publishers, Australia;
'Forebears', by permission of the author; THOMAS
SHAPCOTT: 'The Litanies of Julia Pastrana (1832–1860)' from
Selected Poems (1978), by permission of University of
Queensland Press; R. A. SIMPSON: 'Tram Driver's Song',
'To My Mother' and 'Old Children' from *Selected Poems*
(University of Queensland Press, 1981), by permission of
the author; KENNETH SLESSOR: 'Five Bells' from *Selected
Poems*, copyright © Paul Slessor 1944, by kind permission of
Paul Slessor Collins/Angus & Robertson Publishers,
Australia; 'The Night-Ride', 'Wild Grapes', 'Talbingo',
'Country Towns', 'North Country', 'South Country', 'An
Inscription for Dog River' and 'Beach Burial' from *Selected
Poems*, copyright © Paul Slessor 1944, by permission of
Collins/Angus & Robertson Publishers, Australia; PETER
STEELE: 'Countdown' and 'Element' from *Marching on
Paradise* (1984), by permission of Longman Cheshire Pty Ltd,
Australia; 'Like a Ghost', by permission of the author;
DOUGLAS STEWART: *from* 'Glencoe', 'The Night of the
Moths', 'The Silkworms' and 'B Flat' from *Selected Poems*,
copyright © Margaret Stewart 1973, by permission of
Collins/Angus & Robertson Publishers, Australia;
RANDOLPH STOW: 'Dust', 'Ruins of the City of Hay', 'The
Dying Chair', 'Sleep' and 'Jimmy Woodsers' from *A
Counterfeit Silence* (Angus & Robertson, 1969), copyright ©
Randolph Stow 1969, by permission of Richard Scott Simon
Ltd; JENNIFER STRAUSS: 'After a Death' and 'Stone,
Scissors, Paper' from *Winter Driving* (Sisters, 1981), by
permission of the author; ANDREW TAYLOR: 'Halfway to
Avalon' and 'Two in Search of Dawn' from *Selected Poems
1960–1980* (1982), by permission of University of
Queensland Press; JOHN TRANTER: 'Sonnet 63' *from* 'Crying
in Early Infancy', 'Butterfly' and 'At the Criterion' from
Selected Poems (1982), by permission of Hale & Ironmonger
Pty Ltd, Australia; DIMITRIS TSALOUMAS: 'An Extravagant
Lover's Note of Explanation' and 'The Grudge' from *Falcon
Drinking* (1988), by permission of University of Queensland
Press; CHRIS WALLACE-CRABBE: 'Losses and Recoveries'

Index of Poets

Adamson, Robert, 223

Beaver, Bruce, 136
Blight, John, 53
Buckley, Vincent, 126

Campbell, David, 68
Churches, Christine, 234
Craig, Alexander, 114

Dawe, Bruce, 155
Dobson, Rosemary, 109
Dransfield, Michael, 248

Elder, Anne, 92

Fitzgerald, R. D., 17
Forbes, John, 251

Gray, Robert, 228

Hart, Kevin, 253
Hart-Smith, William, 44
Harwood, Gwen, 99
Hope, A. D., 27

Johnston, Martin, 246
Jones, Evan, 162

Lehmann, Geoffrey, 209

McAuley, James, 87
McDonald, Roger, 217

Mackenzie, Kenneth, 57
McMaster, Rhyll, 239
Malouf, David, 180
Manifold, John, 62
Martin, Philip, 160
Murray, Les A., 193

Neilson, John Shaw, 1

Porter, Peter, 148

Rankin, Jennifer, 215
Riddell, Elizabeth, 39

Shapcott, Thomas, 189
Simpson, R. A., 152
Slessor, Kenneth, 7
Steele, Peter, 207
Stewart, Douglas, 49
Stow, Randolph, 184
Strauss, Jennifer, 166

Taylor, Andrew, 213
Tranter, John, 220
Tsaloumas, Dimitris, 111

Wallace-Crabbe, Chris, 172
Webb, Francis, 116
Wright, Judith, 76

Zwicky, Fay, 169

Index of Titles

Absolutely Ordinary Rainbow, An, 196
Action Would Kill It / A Gamble, 223
Advice to Young Ladies, 34
After a Death, 166
Aftermath: Yorkshire 1644, The, 174
Against the Dark, 89
Against the Wall, 82
Altamira, 47
Ambrosia, 45
Aristarchus and the Whale, 246
Ascent into Hell, 28
At the Criterion, 221
Autumn in Hobart, 91

B Flat, 51
Bachelor Farmer, 218
Bat, 170
Bathymeter, 44
Beach Burial, 16
Bird of Glass, 241
Birth, 45
Blind School, The, 130
Blonde & Aussie, 252
Boundary Conditions, 100
Broad Bean Sermon, The, 199
Buladelah-Taree Holiday Song Cycle, The, 202
Butterfly, 220

Caesura, 58
Ceiling, The, 114
Childhood, 175
Christ of the Abyss, The, 159
Clouds, 155
Coasts of Cerigo, The, 32
Colour Yourself for a Man, 2
Come Back, 256
Conflagration, 54
Cormorants, 53
Countdown, 207
Country Towns, 9
Crazy Woman, 93
Crying in Early Infancy, 220
Curtain, The, 80

Daily Living, 109
Dawn Wind on the Islands, 119
Day of the Statue, The, 116

Death, 1976, 176
Death at Winson Green, A, 123
Death in January, 126
Death of the Bird, The, 31
Dialogue, 87
Dialogue, 106
Disarrayed, The, 55
Divination, 235
Dream in an Afternoon, 242
Dream of France, A, 253
Dream of Washed Hair, A, 242
Dreams, 170
Drifters, 156
Driving through Sawmill Towns, 193
Dust, 184
Dust to Dust, 103
Dying Chair, The, 186

Easiest Room in Hell, The, 149
Easter Hymn, 27
Eeling, 244
Element, 207
Eleven Compositions: Roadside, 20
Evening Alone at Bunyah, 195
Extravagant Lover's Note of Explanation, An, 111

Face of the Waters, The, 18
Falling Sickness, The, 162
Father, Mother, Son, 88
Fencing School, 65
Fife Tune, 64
Fire Screen, 240
Fishing, 44
Five Bells, 11
For a Pastoral Family, 85
For Comrade Katharine, 62
For My Grandfather, 118
For Precision, 80
Forebears, 40

Garden, The, 77
Gateway, The, 27
Glencoe, 49
Golden Builders, 127
Good Ghost, Gaunt Ghost, 151
Grandfather, The, 249
Grandmother's Ninetieth Birthday, 236
Grassfire Stanzas, The, 203
Grasshopper, 217
Growing Up Alone, 226
Grudge, The, 113
Gunner, The, 118

Halfway to Avalon, 213
Hawthorn Hedge, The, 76
Hero and the Hydra, The, *from*, 88
Homecoming, 157
Honeymoon, South Coast, 164
Hostel, 162
Husband and Wife, 156

I Wonder What Went of Him, 237
In the Park, 101
Inscription for a War, 38
Inscription for Dog River, An, 15
Internment, 133

Jasmine, 179
Jesus, 87
Jimmy Woodsers, 188
Journey: the North Coast, 228

Kangaroo, 229

Lachlan MacQuarie's First Language, 201
Lament for the Murderers, 36
Landfall, 72
Landscape, 233
Last Scab of Hawarth, The, 63
Late Summer Storm, 235
Lauds and Plaints, 144
Letter, The, 39
Letters to Live Poets, 136
Like a Ghost, 208
Line from Keats, A, 163
Litanies of Julia Pastrana (1832–1860), 189
Long Since . . ., 17
Looking Towards Bruny, 105
Losses and Recoveries, 172
Loving Kind, 37

Mangrove, 53
Men in Green, 68
Midsummer, 254
Mitchells, The, 200
Morgan's Country, 117
Mother Who Gave Me Life, 107
My Afternoon, 227
My First Proper Girlfriend, 225
My Granny, 224

Neighbour, 234
Nessun Dorma, 124
New Carpentry, 176
Night of the Moths, The, 50

Night-Ride, The, 7
Non Piangere, Liù, 150
North Coast Town, 230
North Country, 9
Nursing Home, 160

Observation, 46
Off the Map, 182
Old Children, 153
Old House, 79
Old Inmate, An, 60
Once Bitten, Twice Bitten; Once Shy, Twice Shy, 148
One Tuesday in Summer, 90
Orange Tree, The, 1
Others, 219

Panoptics, 178
Parish Church, 91
Person to Person, 102
Pioneer Lane, 248
Pleasure of Princes, The, 30
Portents over Coffee, 73
Presences, 250
Prize-Giving, 99
Pro and Con, 83

Reading Horace Outside Sydney: 1970, 181
Real World, The, 255
Rolling in Money, 251
Ross' Poems, 209
Ruins of the City of Hay, 185

Scattering Layer, The, 247
Sea Change, *from*, 114
Sea-Shell, The, 231
Seen Out, 92
Seven in the Morning, 243
Silkworms, The, 50
Singers of Renown, 97
'Single principle of forms, The', 230
Sketch of the Harbour, 232
Slanted World, 239
Sleep, 187
Smalltown Dance, 83
Smell of Coal Smoke, The, 205
Snake, The, 57
Solicitors' World, A, 165
Sonnet, 63, 220
South Country, 10
Starting from Central Station, 71
Still Water Tread, 216
Stone, Scissors, Paper, 167

Stony Town, 4
Sugar Loaf, 72
Sun is Up, The, 3

Take Down the Fiddle, Karl!, 5
Talbingo, 8
Teaching German Literature, 134
This Day, 253
To a Friend under Sentence of Death, 97
To a Sea-Horse, 169
To Another Housewife, 81
To My Mother, 152
Tomb of Lt John Learmonth, AIF, The, 65
Towards the Land of the Composer, 121
Train Journey, 78
Tram Driver's Song, 152
Two in Search of Dawn, 214
Two Songs with Spanish Burdens, 74
Two Trinities, 58

Vlamingh and Rottnest Island, 120

Wade in the Water, 224
Walking in the Lambing Paddock, 238
Walking to the Cattle Place, 197
Washing the Money, 243
Weapons Training, 158
Who Points the Swallow, 69
Wild Grapes, 7
Williamstown, 215
Wind at Your Door, The, 22
Winter Quarters, 104
Woman to Man, 77
Works and Days, 70

Yarra Park, 96
Year of the Foxes, The, 180
Your Father's House, 132
Your Shadow, 255

Index of First Lines

A card comes to tell you, 150
A dry tree with an empty honeycomb, 88
A grasshopper clings crazily, 217
A presence – how can you name a smell?, 179
A world of lunches, conferences behind, 165
After the tide's long gear-shifting gesture, 233
After the whey-faced anonymity, 10
All day a storm has fermented. Now the clouds are huge above the
    mountains, 230
All day, day after day, they're bringing them home, 157
All night headlamps dazzle, 182
All their lives in a box! What generations, 50
Also it could prove serious for the pool, 72
And when I say eyes right I want to hear, 158
Angry-feathered trees, 235
Are you ready? soul said again, 58
At daylight, 255
At half-past five – the earth cooling, 218
At last the night comes, stifling the sun, 250
At the hour I slept, 197
'At the sun's incredible centre', 100
At the top of the stairs is a room, 149
At weekends, my father and younger sister, 243
AUC 334: about this date, 34
August, and black centres expand on the afternoon paddock, 203

Beanstalks, in any breeze, are a slack church parade, 199
Black leather streets are polished by the fog, 214
Bonewhite the newborn flesh, the crucified, 91
Boosting the hula hoop, fates, 252
Born bat-blind, 170
Bottle-brush is best, it likes sweet water, 235

'Check it in here,' he said, 176
Christmas – always, forever, a Morning and a Coming, 120
Come back to me, 256
Country towns, with your willows and squares, 9
Creases of the shouldery mountain, 175

Death when he walks behind me frightens me, 83
Do you remember how we went, 81
Do you remember the peacocks, 241

'Enough,' she said. But the dust still rained about her, 184
Erskineville. The sun came round a corner, 248
Even if there'd been prayers, 127
Eyes on the plate – the scoop of mashed potato, 162

Fishing skiff in the light, 226
Flexed suddenly the muscles of the stomach, 251
Flowers of red silk and purple velvet grew, 77
For every bird there is this last migration, 31
Forgetting how to observe, what, 55
From the domed head the defeated eyes peer out, 88
Frost on the ground, 240

Gas flaring on the yellow platform; voices running up and down, 7
Glassed with cold sleep and dazzled by the moon, 78
God knows what was done to you, 136
Green sweater a little rubbed, 114

Half of the land, conscious of love and grief, 32
Having said that all the gums have not been cut, 20
He feared angina from his thirtieth year, 71
Heads moved in a wide, slow, semi-circle, 44
He lifted a drop of ambrosia, 45
How long ago she planted the hawthorn hedge, 76

I am always here leaning against the fog, 155
I am seeing this: two men are sitting on a pole, 200
I cannot resist now and then being born, 45
I don't go down to the pub much any more, 221
I dream I stand once more, 103
I know him only as a man of Sunday afternoon, and a backyard fire
    burning, 234
I listen each week to the discs, 97
I rose to catch the early morning, 239
I saw its periscope in the tide, 53
I Stop. I go again, 152
I take my pen in hand, 39
I teach German Literature, and this is how it goes, 134
I think of sex all afternoon, 227
I, too, at the mid-point, in a well-lit wood, 28
If an angel came with one wish, 106
If I ever go to Stony town, I'll go as to a fair, 4
In a distant field, small animals prepare, 220
In a hollow where late-mown pasture lapses to straw, 105
In about a week, they say, 97
In early ear oats glaze; wheat is hard green, 70
In here it's seven o'clock, 243
In the high cool country, 193
In the waters off Portofino, 159
In these few wire-taut weeks, 176
Incontinence, and the mind going. Where?, 160
Inside the gates his drive is a chain of ponds. the car stalls, 249
It is coming up, 72
It was another race, 178
It was the curtain, softly rising and falling, 80

Joe Green Joe Green O how are you doing today?, 60

John Brown, glowing far and down, 205

Knocking his knuckles against the wall, 82

Last night I dreamt of the Pittsburgh tunnels, 166
Let us, to pass the time as we cycle, 246
Life to be understood turns into legend, 89
Linger not, stranger, shed no tear, 38
Long since I heard the muttered anger of the reef, 17
Love who points the swallow home, 69
Loving Kind went by the way, 37
Lying with my back on the slanted weir, 242

Make no mistake; there will be no forgiveness, 27
Men openly call you the enemy, call you the swine, 5
Mother who gave me life, 107
Me ancestor was called on to go out, 22
My mother has lived, 152

Next thing, I wake up in a swaying bunk, 228
No longer glimpsing a few beer cans that glint, 114
No place was like your father's house. I followed, 132
North Country, filled with gesturing wood, 9
Now and then concentrating, 46
Now the heart sings with all its thousand voices, 27

O Search the heart and belly you may find, 40
Often, among the night-sounds, I've heard, 126
On the first day of autumn Euterpe called to me, 93
Once again the scurry of feet – those myriads, 18
One day soon he'll tell her it's time to start packing, 156
One held the resined pinebranch, 47
One morning in spring, 64
Our general was the greatest and bravest of generals, 15
Out beside the highway, first thing in the morning, 230

Past six o'clock, I have prayed. No one is sleeping, 124
Pearlised shadows, 244
Praying to you can be talking to the sea, 207
Professor Eisenbart, asked to attend, 99

Rain tries the one small foot and at length the other, 121
Rain walks all night across the greenhouse roof, 247
Rasps with crying. All night, 130
Rays of sunlight quietly fishing from tall trees, 255
Remembering. Pools. Remembering. Eyes. Remembering, 188
Restless at night and during storms, 253

She is coming towards me, 151
She sits in the park. Her clothes are out of date, 101
Sigh, wind in the pine, 49
Sing softly, Muse, the Reverend Henry White, 51

Sitting on the divan, 111
Sleep: you are my homestead, and my garden, 187
Sleeping badly, he'd wake in a rage, 170
Snow-cloud, a rainbow, blue sky, rain, 91
So we meet as of old where the rosevine, 102
Softly and humbly to the Gulf of Arabs, 16
Some of them evil, most good, 92
Sometime shortly after the rain began, 164
Sometimes at night when the heart stumbles and stops, 58
Speak not of Death: it is a merry morn, 3
Standing under the shower, 242
Strange that your image should occur to me, 113

'Talbingo River' – as one says of bones, 8
Talked to the wife and children, talked to the man, 208
That hungry face, 229
That moment on my mind, 62
That Spring I was twelve, 238
That sultry afternoon the world went strange, 90
The clock above stalled traffic, white as bread, 253
The distance is deceptive. Sydney glitters invisible, 181
The eyeless labourer in the night, 77
The first girl I wanted to marry, 225
The foliage of light begins to wither, 162
The giant moths like sparrows! So many drowned, 50
*The Governor and the seer are talking at night in a room beyond formality. They are
    not speaking English*, 201
The long, wet trajectory of the ferry's railing, 232
The Lord's name be praised, 189
The man raced wildly through a burning, 54
The motor died with an underwater cough, 213
The needle of dawn has drugged them, life and death, 119
The old jokes aren't as funny as they were, 156
The old orchard, full of smoking air, 7
The Park at the arse end of Winter, 96
The sea has it this way: if you see, 53
The seers may chasten; the fools may bid the waters dance uphill, 2
The south-coast sun, the play of light and air, 163
The stars of the holiday step out all over the sky, 202
The stick, the fan, the basket, the morning paper, 109
The thin brown house waits with me, 215
The trap setter in a steel dawn, 148
The wind has scattered my city to the sheep, 185
The word goes round Repins, 196
The young girl stood beside me, 1
Then there was cool dispersion everywhere, 174
There he goes, went, catch him, 172
There is a glow in the kitchen window now, 195
There is a green spell stolen from Birmingham, 123
There was a pattering in the rafters, mother, 87
There were fifteen men in green, 68
These are the richest weeks, 254

They have him squeezed into the square room, 133
They wander near the estuary, 153
This is Morgan's country: now steady, Bill, 117
This is not sorrow, this is work: I build, 65
Those who have descended to the nethermost deeps, 44
Time that is moved by little fidget wheels, 11
To stand hushed an hour or so, 144
Touching Ezekiel his workman's hand, 87
Turtles hatch in the hot sands, 73
Twisting words into slow shape, 237
Two women find the square-root of a sheet, 83

Vadoga, my middle-aged brother, 186

Wall-eyed snouter, sweet feeble translucent, 169
We cover the hole in the ground, 236
We sit in someone else's house, 104
What pleasures have great princes? These: to know, 30
When all the rivers turn back again in our time, 224
When I couldn't he always discussed things, 223
When I was ten my mother, having sold, 180
When my Granny was dying, 224
When she was fourteen, she says, 220
When the gunner spoke in his sleep the hut was still, 118
When the ropes droop and loosen, and the gust, 118
Where are they now, the genteel murderers, 36
Where now outside the weary house the pepperina, 79
White as crockery, 231
White to the neck he glides and plunges, 65
Who are you to unsettle me?, 216
Who of those asleep at midnight over blank television screens, 219
Why does the fire burn high to me, 63
Why is the face of the dead so absolute, 167
Winter blows itself out with quick cloud and white sunshine, 74
With hours to go before the Long Retreat, 207
Withdrawing from the amorous grasses, 57

Yet a marginal sort of grace, 85
Yet I go on from day to day, betraying, 80
You can't hear it in the house, 209
You look for prodigies leaning on the sill of storm, 116
You swing when ready. Holding, 252

[275]